As one of the world's longest established
and best-known travel brands,
Thomas Cook are the experts in travel.

For more than 135 years our
guidebooks have unlocked the secrets
of destinations around the world,
sharing with travellers a wealth of
experience and a passion for travel.

**Rely on Thomas Cook as your
travelling companion on your next trip
and benefit from our unique heritage.**

Thomas Cook **traveller** guides

SEYCHELLES
Katerina Roberts

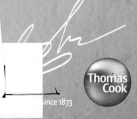

since 1873

Written and updated by Katerina Roberts
Original photography by Eric Roberts

Published by Thomas Cook Publishing
A division of Thomas Cook Tour Operations Limited
Company registration no. 3772199 England
The Thomas Cook Business Park, Unit 9, Coningsby Road,
Peterborough PE3 8SB, United Kingdom
Email: books@thomascook.com, Tel: +44 (0) 1733 416477
www.thomascookpublishing.com

Produced by Cambridge Publishing Management Limited
Burr Elm Court, Main Street, Caldecote CB23 7NU
www.cambridgepm.co.uk

ISBN: 978-1-84848-395-8

© 2007, 2009 Thomas Cook Publishing
This third edition © 2011
Text © Thomas Cook Publishing
Maps © Thomas Cook Publishing/PCGraphics (UK) Limited

Series Editor: Karen Beaulah
Production/DTP: Steven Collins

Printed and bound in Spain by GraphyCems

Cover photography © Photononstop/SuperStock

Contents

Introduction

Scattered over 1,400,000sq km (54,000sq miles) of the western Indian Ocean, the 115 islands that make up the Seychelles archipelago offer visitors some of the most beautiful and unspoiled destinations on earth.

An environmentally friendly holiday haven

The pristine beaches framed by swaying palm trees, a pleasant year-round climate, and a country that is a treasure trove of unique flora and fauna are the biggest draws for visitors to these shores. With just under half of the land mass given over to national parks, marine parks and special reserves, it's no surprise that Seychelles scores high on the environmental front thanks to sustainable environmental management policies that benefit visitors and islanders alike.

One of the most important decisions to make when considering a holiday in the Seychelles is where to base yourself. There are 18 islands offering eco-friendly accommodation, from the granitic islands of Mahé, Praslin and La Digue in the Inner Islands group to the coral atolls of the Outer Islands, which are tailor-made for nature- and sea-lovers and the undeniably romantic.

Islands within islands

Whether you stay in Mahé or island-hop, Seychelles has something for everyone. The biggest of the islands, Mahé, offers superb beaches, trekking in the misty mountains of the Morne Seychellois National Park, plus shopping and snapshots of its colonial past in the capital, Victoria. On Praslin, you can play castaway on one of the world's best beaches or take a spooky walk through a mysterious forest that is also a UNESCO World Heritage Site. And on La Digue, you can bike, hike or ox-cart your way through jungly forest paths or just lap up the island's laid-back lifestyle.

For pure escapism, Desroches and Alphonse in the Outer Islands, over 1,600km (1,000 miles) from anywhere, feel like the edge of the world. For sporty types, there's diving and fishing to take your breath away, and magnificent beaches on which to cast away your woes. Then there is Aldabra, the largest raised coral atoll in the

A picture-postcard beach on Desroches Island

world, declared a UNESCO World Heritage Site and one of the few places on earth where giant land tortoises dominate the terrestrial fauna.

Culture and cuisine

With a diverse population drawn from just over two centuries of history, shaped by French and British settlers, African and Malagasy slaves and Asian immigrants, the Seychellois are remarkably westernised compared with other island nations in the region yet still maintain their cultural roots. A charming easy-going lifestyle, no racial tension, a politically stable government and a relatively safe and crime-free environment are just some of the reasons why visitors return.

Gourmets will find the islands' food heaven, particularly if fond of fish. Wherever you dine, fresh-caught fish spiked with herbs and spices, delicious curries and a dazzling array of exotic fruits and vegetables are spread in a gargantuan feast before your eyes.

It would take a lifetime to experience all the islands, but then Seychelles is the sort of destination that you leave wanting to return. It's one of those rare places where megabytes are what giant tortoises take at dinner, networking is the domain of fishermen, and if you go to one of those faraway islands like Desroches, Alphonse, Denis or Bird, it's worth remembering that your mobile phone simply won't work. Welcome to the Seychelles!

The land

The Seychelles is made up of 43 Inner Islands and 72 Outer Islands, lying between latitude 4 degrees south and 10 degrees south and between longitude 46 degrees east and 54 degrees east. The Inner Islands, which include Mahé, Praslin and La Digue, are approximately 1,600km (1,000 miles) east of Africa. They are the oldest oceanic islands in the world (750 million years) and the only islands not formed from undersea volcanic or coralline activity.

A lost continent

It's almost certain that Seychelles was originally a part of the Indian/Eurasian continent before intense sub-oceanic movement tore it away and stranded it in mid-ocean. Then Seychelles was a lump of lifeless granite, about the size of Great Britain, until it was slowly eroded by wind and water over millions of years. With the rise of sea levels and the weight of the carbonate platform supporting coral reefs, the total land occupied by the granitics is now little more than 110sq km (42sq miles) or one-thousandth of its original size.

By contrast, a drop in sea levels, a mere few thousand years ago, has exposed the outer coral islands. The shallow seas reveal sandy banks that have developed into often strange horseshoe shapes of raised coral islands encompassing limpid lagoons. The lagoons are nearly empty at low tide, so that you can almost pick your own fish.

A thousand miles from everywhere

The main reason that Seychelles has only been inhabited for just over 200 years must surely be its remoteness from the rest of the world. Scattered as they are over 455sq km (176sq miles), and with Mahé over 1,600km (1,000 miles) from the mainland of India and the same distance from Africa and Madagascar, it's understandable that nobody bothered to make anything of a settlement in these islands, if only from the logistical travelling point of view. Mid-ocean isolation has also been a major factor in the preservation of the islands in their pristine condition. Until the late 18th century, no human hand had touched the islands for more than a fleeting moment.

The best example of a remote tropical garden and habitat of animal and marine life is Aldabra. This, the largest raised coral atoll in the world, is home to more than 150,000 giant tortoises which have lived and

The land

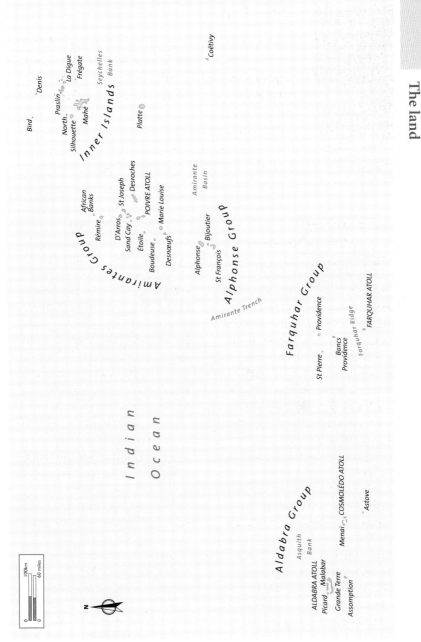

Inner Islands

Bird
Denis
Praslin
La Digue
Frégate
North
Silhouette
Mahé
Seychelles Bank
Platte
Coëtivy

Amirantes Group

African Banks
Rémire
D'Arros
St Joseph
Sand Cay
Desroches
Étoile
POIVRE ATOLL
Boudeuse
Marie Louise
Desnœufs
Amirante Basin

Alphonse Group

Alphonse
Bijoutier
St François
Amirante Trench

Farquhar Group

St Pierre
Providence
Bancs Providence
Farquhar Ridge
FARQUHAR ATOLL

Aldabra Group

Asquith Bank
Menai
COSMOLÉDO ATOLL
Astove
ALDABRA ATOLL
Picard
Malabar
Grande Terre
Assomption

Indian Ocean

0   100km
0   60 miles

N

bred successfully on the inhospitable terrain that has been their saviour against settlement by humans. Turtles, tortoises, birds and millions of fish in the 34sq km (13sq miles) of lagoon have been left to proliferate in blissful seclusion. Even today there are only transient visitors, a few scientists, a warden and staff occupying small houses from which they monitor data and help protect this unique habitat. Aldabra is the furthest outpost of Seychelles, untouched and rarely visited, a perfect land in a perfect animal world where the only footprints are those of birds and tortoises.

Lagoons are an important feature in the geography of the Seychelles

History

9th–10th centuries	Arab traders speak of 'a high island' beyond the Maldives that appears on Arab charts as Zarin (The Sisters).
1502–3	Explorers João da Nova and Vasco da Gama sail near what are now known as the Farquhar and Amirantes Islands and plot them on Portuguese charts.
1609	English trading ship *Ascension* visits Mahé to make the first recorded landing, but the islands remain uninhabited.
Late 17th–early 18th centuries	Pirates from Saint Mary's island near Madagascar use Seychelles as a base for raiding passing East India merchant ships.
1742	Mahé de Labourdonnais, the governor of Mauritius, sends Lazare Picault to chart the islands. Picault names the largest island Mahé.
1756	Captain Corneille Nicolas Morphy claims the islands for France and names them Seychelles after the French minister of finance.
1770–78	French entrepreneur Brayer du Barré arrives with first settlers. Pierre Poivre establishes the Royal Spice Garden and the first buildings are erected at L'Etablissement du Roi (Victoria). Slaves imported from Africa and Madagascar.
1790	The first administrative colonial assembly is formed under Queneau de Quincy as the French Commandant.
1793–1812	Quincy sees the islands through the years of war between France and Britain, and guides Seychelles through prosperous years trading with both the French and British. He signs a capitulation treaty, the first of seven during this period.
1815	Seychelles becomes a British colony under the Treaty of Paris 1814.
1835	Slavery is abolished.
1839	Full emancipation of slaves completed.

1841 L'Etablissement renamed Victoria. Seychelles' population tops 5,000 and coconut plantations are established.

1861 First liberated African slaves arrive and work the land for wages.

1862 An avalanche falls on Victoria, killing 60 people.

1890–1900 Coconut oil reaches record production levels. Vanilla and cloves become popular cash crops.

1903 Seychelles becomes a British Crown Colony independent from Mauritius.

1906 Vanilla prices fall but coconut oil remains the mainstay, and increased world demand for vanilla boosts the economy.

1914–18 World War I leaves Seychelles deprived of supplies. The Seychelles Pioneer Corps serves with the British in East Africa.

1926 Electricity and telephone services commence to serve a population of 24,000.

1929 The Colonial Development Act ensures a more liberal flow of funds despite the economic recession.

1937 League of Coloured Peoples formed to represent plantation workers. Minimum wage established.

1939 The Seychelles Tax Payers Association formed to represent the planters against colonial administration.

1939–45 During World War II, the Seychelles Pioneer Corps serves alongside British troops. Allied ships and seaplanes use Sainte Anne island for refuelling.

1964 Two political parties are created, the Seychelles People's United Party (SPUP) led by Albert René, and the Seychelles Democratic Party (SDP) led by James Mancham.

1965 British Indian Ocean Territory (BIOT) from some outlying Seychelles islands is formed.

1967 Universal adult suffrage introduced.

1970	First Legislative Assembly established.	**1992**	After exile in Britain, Mancham returns. He reconciles with René and a multi-party system is restored.
1971	Mahé International Airport opens and tourism takes off.		
1976	Seychelles becomes an independent republic within the Commonwealth and is governed by a coalition of SPUP/SDP parties with Mancham as president and René as prime minister. In 1977, while Mancham attends a conference in London, René organises a coup and becomes president, calling himself an Indian-Ocean socialist.	**1993**	René continues as president following first elections under the new constitution.
		1998	René wins a three-way election between his SPPF, the SNP and Mancham's SDP, with Mancham coming in last.
		2000–2003	SPPF continues in power. René cites James Alix Michel, his longest-serving cabinet minister, as his successor.
1979	René imposes a new constitution that allows a single-party system led by his Seychelles People Progressive Front (SPPF).	**2004**	Elections result in James Alix Michel as president.
1981	An attempted coup led by the mercenary Major 'Mad Mike' Hoare is quashed at the airport. Mancham denies any involvement.	**2009–11**	International attention focuses on increasing attacks by Somalian pirates. Seychelles signs piracy agreements with Kenya, USA and EU and becomes second regional centre for prosecution of pirates. First piracy trial results in 11 Somalians sentenced to 10 years with 29 suspects awaiting trial.
1982	A mutiny by the Seychelles Army is quelled by Tanzanian troops.		
1984–9	René is twice re-elected president.		

World's best beaches

Dazzling white beaches, swaying palms, shaded *takamaka* trees and calm blue waters conspire to justify all the clichés used in holiday travel brochures, and it's not surprising that Seychelles scores high in the beauty stakes. In 2010 Seychelles ranked among the Top 10 Best Ethical Destinations of the developing world for its environment protection measures by *Ethical Traveller*. *Condé Nast*, meanwhile, put Seychelles at number six in their Top Islands award and was voted as the Most Environmentally Friendly destination in their annual readers' awards.

Anse Intendance in Mahé

Nature works hard at giving the Seychelles such beautiful beaches, but sometimes it turns aggressive. Few people sunning themselves on the sparkling sands of **Anse Lazio** on Plasliin would believe that the tsunami, which swept across the Indian Ocean in 2004, caused the bay to empty, exposing the sea floor, before crashing across the road and damaging a beachside restaurant. The tsunami was so powerful that it even wiped out La Reserve Hotel in the secluded cove of **Anse Petite Cour** in the north of the island, and the hotel had to be rebuilt from scratch.

Today, Anse Lazio and that other dream beach of **Anse Source d'Argent** on La Digue (*see p77*) are just as nature intended, and people make special trips here just to laze, snorkel and swim. Even on grey and overcast days, many visitors return to their hotels agreeing that these beaches are the world's best, and that the hype is most certainly true.

Other beaches in Mahé that deserve the 'best beach' accolade are **Beau Vallon** (*see p44*) for its year-round calm waters that make it safe for swimming and watersports, and **Anse Intendance** on the southwest

No sign of the 2004 tsunami at Anse Lazio now

coast which is dominated by the celebrity-starred Banyan Tree Resort. Anse Intendance has a rugged beauty, especially during the southeast monsoon when giant rollers pound ashore, but at other times the ocean takes on the appearance of glistening glass. You don't have to be a guest of the Banyan Tree to enjoy this beach either. Coming from the north, just drive past the hotel entrance where a track on the right leads to a carpet of white sand.

The beach at **Anse Soleil** on Mahé's southwest coast was voted as 'second best hidden secret' in the world by German magazine, *Reise und Preise*, and understandably so. Sometimes you feel like you're going through hell to reach paradise as you drive along a 3km (1¾-mile) steep bumpy track bounded by dense jungly vegetation just west from Baie Lazare. However, the journey's end reveals a gem, a truly well-kept secret known only to guests staying at the Anse Soleil Beachcomber Hotel, where the adjacent café provides welcome snacks.

East from Anse Soleil is **Anse à la Mouche**, a deep sheltered bay, yet to receive a 'best beach' award. If all you want to do is pad barefoot along soft sands, maybe toe-dip in the shallow lagoon or people-watch over a cool drink in the Anchor Café on the seafront, then, for some, this must rank as the most perfect beach in the world.

Politics

For a young island state inhabited by people from diverse cultures and religions, the Seychelles archipelago has enjoyed a stable and relatively trouble-free existence since independence from Great Britain in 1976.

In the run-up to independence, many Seychellois felt disgruntled with British colonial rule and realised that the country needed to focus on its economic future. With James Mancham as leader, education and prosperity beyond the basic island subsistence level seemed attainable.

In the mid-1960s, two political parties were formed – the Seychelles Democratic Party (SDP) of James Mancham and the Seychelles People's United Party (SPUP) of Albert René. René was a socialist keen on independence from Great Britain, whereas Mancham wanted to keep firm ties with the mother country. In 1967, a legislative council was formed and adult suffrage introduced. In elections, Mancham narrowly won, by a small percentage over René, the right to become chief minister. By the 1970s, an international airport was being built and the prospect of Seychelles' identity as a tourist destination was in sight.

After independence in 1976, René's SPUP and Mancham's SDP formed a coalition government. Mancham became president and René was prime minister. The honeymoon didn't last long. The following year, while Mancham was in London attending the Commonwealth Conference, René and his supporters in the military staged a coup d'état. Mancham remained in Great Britain and René announced a one-party state that lasted 25 years.

René's time in power was not altogether peaceful. In 1981, Major 'Mad Mike' Hoare led a group of mercenaries masquerading as tourists from South Africa. They were thwarted at Mahé airport and they escaped in a hijacked plane. Three years later, Gerald Hoareau, founder of a resistance movement, was released from prison and moved to London only to be found shot dead outside his home. The crime was never solved but he became a martyr to the cause of the opposition.

In 1992, Mancham made a comeback to the Seychelles with his new Democratic Party and the country returned to multi-party politics. At the first election in 1993, René still managed to win and, as Mancham's popularity waned, René continued to scrape through and win every election until 2003 when he transferred power to the then vice-president, James Alix Michel. Michel became president in the 2004 elections.

Michel's ambition is to steer a path that capitalises on the success of the last decade. Tourism is the mainstay of the economy and, despite the global recession, 2009 ended with just a one per cent drop in visitor arrivals. The year 2010 brought about a strong working partnership between the government under President Michel and the tourism industry, resulting in new markets in China, South Korea and Lebanon.

The 81,000 Seychellois enjoy a stable middle-class standard of living and good health and social security benefits. However, with everything being imported, prices are higher than in Europe. The government aims to encourage small businesses and to provide education and training in skills to enable the country to become more productive and self-sufficient. Real-estate projects and tax incentives are also in place, including residential status for foreign investors.

The Desroches Island home of Albert René, an important figure in Seychelles politics

Culture

The Seychelles people are a pot-pourri of nations. Their cultural roots stem from African and Malagasy slaves brought by French settlers, British colonists and Asian immigrants. What unites them is a short history of just under 250 years and a common Seychellois identity reflected in music, language, folklore and tradition.

Music and dancing

The Seychellois love to sing and dance. They're just as happy dressing up to let their hair down in a modern nightclub as they are donning shorts and a vest to dance a traditional *moutya* around a fire on the beach. The *moutya* blends African and Malagasy rhythms in an erotic dance form that can be performed spontaneously or at an organised cultural show. At these shows, traditional stringed musical instruments, such as the *zez*, *bonm* or *makalapo*, are played, but you are more likely to hear the drumbeat of the *tam tam*. Other dances might include the *masok* and *kosez* – variations of the waltz and the quadrille, which were handed down from the early French settlers.

Language and literature

Creole is the lingua franca, and until it was made an official language in 1981, very little literature existed, mainly because there was no standardised spelling system. The Creole Institute was set up by the government to promote the use of Creole by developing a dictionary, sponsoring literary competitions, giving instruction in translation, and preparing material to teach Creole to foreigners. Some foreign works have been translated into Creole but books written in Creole have yet to be translated into English.

Traditional *moutya* dance

A local artist, Marday, captures everyday life in the Seychelles

Folklore and legend

For many years, superstition and folklore featured strongly in people's lives, and myths still surround the potency of black magic or *gris gris*. Black magic was imported by slaves who would dream up potions for love or revenge. Although banned in 1958, the practice still goes on, particularly among older folk who consult a *bonhomn dibwa* (medicine man) when their luck is up or down.

Slaves would rely on plants and herbs to cure their ills, and this knowledge was handed down through the generations. Even today, especially on islands where there are no hospitals, people resort to nature's medicine chest. Lemon grass, drunk as an infusion, is a stomach settler, and there are various herbs to treat liver complaints, sore throats and headaches. Even the harmless palm spider has its uses, and a Seychellois, with no recourse to a doctor or hospital, wouldn't think twice about removing the legs, heating up the body and using it as a poultice to treat a troublesome boil!

Images of the national psyche

The best place to meet the Seychellois and share their joie de vivre, food and culture is at the Labrin Market (*see p48*) on Wednesday and the last Saturday of the month at Beau Vallon. It is here that you can relate the symbolism of their national flag with its oblique bands of colour to the national psyche. Blue is for the sky and the sea, yellow for the sun that gives light and life, red for the people and their determination to work for the future in unity and love, white for social justice and harmony, and green for the land and natural environment.

Ecotourism

The Seychelles welcomed 160,000 visitors in 2009, and by 2017 hopes to increase this to 350,000. Yet for all the pressures on its resources, it remains one of the most beautiful and unspoiled destinations on earth. Protection of the environment was recognised as far back as the 1970s when the government brought in legislation to establish national parks and marine reserves.

A policy of sustainable environmental management aims to ensure that the Seychellesois continue to conserve their natural heritage. Over half of the country's land mass is monitored and protected, thus preserving its unique ecosystem for future generations. Heavy investment goes into maintaining the national parks and reserves, and much of the work is undertaken by the private sector and non-governmental organisations (NGOs).

A treasure house of flora and fauna

The country has over 1,000 endemic species of flora, over 75 species of fauna and 15 species of birds. There are 20 national parks and reserves as well as two UNESCO World Heritage Sites – the Vallée de Mai on Praslin where the unique forest of *coco de mer* palm thrives, and Aldabra Atoll, home to a unique ecosystem and of tremendous importance to scientists.

Eco-friendly islands

Visiting Aldabra and the Outer Islands (*see pp110–11*) may be a mere pipe dream for some because they are so expensive to access, but nearer to Mahé there are many islands that are prime examples of responsible ecotourism projects. On Silhouette and Curieuse, visitors and volunteers can take part in giant land tortoise captivity breeding programmes run by Nature Protection Trust Seychelles. Other islands are home to privately managed small resorts, such as Bird, Denis, North and Frégate, with accommodation built to strict guidelines and recreational facilities designed to cause minimum impact on the environment.

Cousin, run by Nature Seychelles, and Aride, run by the Royal Society for Nature Conservation, are further examples of how tourism sits comfortably alongside nature. Rules and regulations are in place to ensure that visitors remain eco-friendly by not smoking, not taking away any plants or animals, and leaving no litter behind. By visiting these islands, you are not only playing an active role in non-invasive ecotourism activities, such as birdwatching and nature trail walking, but also helping to fund vital conservation work.

Diving with gentle giants

Dive centres, such as **Underwater Centre Seychelles** in Mahé (*Beau Vallon; tel: 345 445*), offer whale shark encounters. These 10m (33ft) giants are hunted in the Indian Ocean but are a protected species in Seychelles waters. You can combine an exciting diving itinerary and swim with them, or join a 45-minute trip in a microlight with a research team from the Seychelles Marine Conservation Society to record observations, but do book well in advance.

Clean and green

Islanders themselves are mindful of the need to keep the environment clean for everyone to enjoy. You'd be hard pushed to find litter in the capital, Victoria, and wherever you go, whether it's to the famous beaches of Anse Lazio on Praslin or Anse Source d'Argent on La Digue, or some nameless cove on a faraway island, you won't find tin cans or

You can help out at a giant land tortoise breeding programme

plastic bottles polluting the beach, or even a garbage bin. That's because Seychellois beachgoers take home with them the detritus of modern living, leaving the coast to be washed by nature's gentle hand.

Festivals and events

Sailing, fishing and diving are some of the main reasons for going to the Seychelles, and it's understandable that these activities are being developed into major events along with festivals celebrating Creole culture and music.

February
The low-key Hindu festival of Kavadi Thaipoosum is celebrated in February.

March
International Carnival
Seychelles' first international carnival takes place in 2011. Representatives from the world's most prestigious carnivals and locals crowd Victoria with colourful floats for this three-day festival.

Sailing is attracting visitors to events such as the Seychelles Sailing Cup

Further details from the tourist office (see pp28–9).

April
National Fishing Tournament
This weekend-long trolling and bottom fishing tournament starts from Victoria.
Further details from Marine Charter Association. Tel: 513 475; email: mca@seychelles.net

May
Fetafrik
This multi-artistic festival of African and Creole culture celebrates Africa Day on 25 May. Regional artistes pump up the action with performances held mainly in Mahé. For details on venues and where to buy tickets contact the tourist office (*see pp28–9*).

Seychelles Regatta
This is a major attraction for visitors coming to Seychelles during May. The event, organised by the Seychelles Tourist

Board in partnership with private sponsors, is a thrilling week of serious competition limited to 20 international teams who sail the Inner Islands.
Details and entry form at www.theseychelles.regatta.com

August
Feast of the Assumption of Mary
Held on 15 August with the main celebrations held on La Digue.

South East Monsoon Sailfish Tournament
A one-day trolling event from Victoria Harbour in Mahé.
Further details and entry form from Marine Charter Association, Victoria. Tel: 322 126. Tournament rules from christophe.houareau@huntdeltel.com

October
Festival Kreol The end of October is the time when the Seychellois let their hair down. Festival Kreol is a celebration of Seychellois and Creole identity, with artistes from other Creole countries such as Mauritius, Réunion and the Caribbean joining in a five-day festival of song, dance, food-tasting and colourful processions. Many activities are held at hotels and on the beaches in Mahé, Praslin and La Digue.
www.Seychelles.net/festivalkreol

SUBIOS Underwater Film and Image Festival
This festival attracts film-makers, photographers, ecologists and

Get some practice in for the fishing competition

journalists to a week's celebration of Seychelles' underwater world with an exciting programme of photographic competitions and presentations by experts. It not only highlights Seychelles as a diving destination, but also raises local awareness of the fragility of the underwater world in schools and colleges. Many events held at hotels are aimed at visitors and local people with a special interest in diving and the marine world.
www.subios.com

November
Marlin Fishing Tournament
Trolling and big-game fishing competition starting from Victoria Harbour in Mahé.
Further details from Marine Charter Association, Victoria. Tel: 513 475.

Highlights

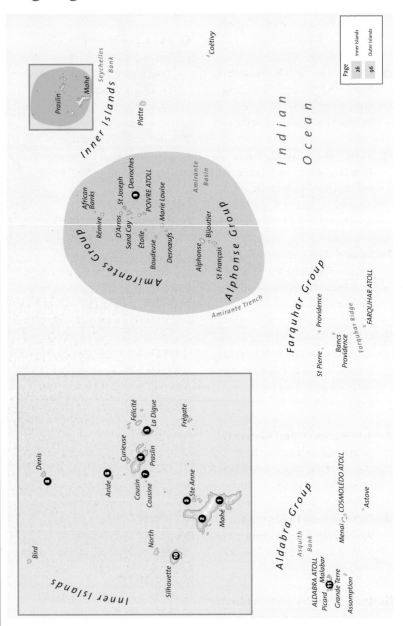

Inner Islands

Seychelles Bank

Praslin

Mahé

Platte

Indian Ocean

Amirantes Group

African Banks

Rémire

D'Arros

St Joseph

Desroches

Sand Cay

POIVRE ATOLL

Étoile

Boudeuse

Marie Louise

Desnœufs

Amirante Basin

Alphonse

Bijoutier

St François

Alphonse Group

Amirante Trench

Farquhar Group

St Pierre

Providence

Bancs Providence

Farquhar Ridge

FARQUHAR ATOLL

Coëtivy

Page	
26	Inner Islands
96	Outer Islands

Inner Islands

Bird

Denis

Aride 6

North

Curieuse

Félicité

Cousin 7

Praslin 4

La Digue 5

Silhouette 10

Cousine

Frégate

Ste Anne 3

Mahé 2 1

Aldabra Group

Asquith Bank

Menai

COSMOLÉDO ATOLL

Astove

ALDABRA ATOLL

Picard

Malabar 11

Grande Terre

Assomption

❶ Mahé Marvel at Mahé's hidden attractions, including one of the world's smallest capitals, Victoria (*see pp26–51*).

❷ Morne Seychellois National Park Explore mist forests and walking trails in the Morne Seychellois National Park (*see pp39–41*).

❸ Sainte Anne National Marine Park Discover colourful corals and the islands in the Sainte Anne National Marine Park off Mahé's east coast (*see pp52–7*).

❹ Vallée de Mai Visit the primeval forests of Vallée de Mai on Praslin, a UNESCO World Heritage Site (*see pp64–5*).

❺ La Digue Island-hop to La Digue for its laid-back lifestyle, elegant plantation houses and stunningly beautiful sandy beaches (*see pp74–7*).

❻ Aride Special Nature Reserve Get close to nature on Aride Bird Reserve, the seabird capital of the Indian Ocean (*see pp70–71*).

❼ Cousin Nature Reserve Cruise to this bird sanctuary, a treasure trove for bird and wildlife enthusiasts (*see pp71–2*).

❽ Denis Island Fly to Denis Island for a desert island experience, and insights into ecotourism (*see pp84–7*).

❾ Desroches Island Dive off Desroches Island in the far-off Amirantes Group, and come face to face with marine life (*see pp102–3*).

❿ Silhouette Slow down on Silhouette where tortoises determine the pace of life (*see pp88–9*).

⓫ Aldabra Atoll Find the world's end at Aldabra Atoll, Seychelles' premier UNESCO World Heritage Site (*see pp110–11*).

Anse Marron, La Digue

Suggested itineraries

The Seychelles has lots to keep you entertained, whether you have just a few days or a few weeks to explore. You can observe wildlife in its natural habitat, go hiking in the beautiful national parks, wander around the bustling towns or just chill out on the stunning white-sand beaches.

Long weekend

Privately owned Denis Island is the perfect getaway if you have a long weekend to spare, and it is only a 30-minute flight from Mahé. As the plane comes in to land, you are treated to a magnificently bright, beach-belted green island, seemingly a million miles from anywhere.

You can stroll around the island in less than two hours. Better still, join a nature tour with the island's conservation officer for an informative account of how this island has become virtually self-sufficient, making full use of natural resources, and growing produce for the only place to stay on the island, the Denis Island Resort.

The Denis Island Resort (*see p82*) offers barefoot luxury in a totally safe environment. It's the kind of place where you literally kick off your shoes, divorce yourself from work because your Blackberry won't work, and with no key supplied for your room, you don't even have to worry about locking yourself out.

One week
Mahé

Mahé is the biggest island in the Seychelles, and home to one of the world's tiniest capitals, Victoria. Most people base themselves at the tourist beach of Beau Vallon on the west coast, but wherever you stay, getting around is easy. Walkers can explore trails with or without a guide in the gorgeous Morne Seychellois National Park or take a magnificent coastal trek from Danzilles to Anse Major beach, recovering with a welcome swim in turquoise waters or hopping aboard a catamaran for a cruise back to Victoria.

For insights into what makes the Seychellois tick, spend at least half a day in busy little Victoria taking in the Botanical Gardens, museums and colourful market, or organise some island-hopping from the tour and boat operators based here.

Unmissable is a boat trip to the Sainte Anne Marine Park to discover bright corals, and views of Mahé from the sea, just as the first sailors did. Then, maybe enjoy a tasty Creole barbecue lunch at the minuscule islands of Moyenne or Cerf.

Mahé's 70-odd beaches are definitely worth exploring, especially down at Anse Intendance, Anse Takamaka, Anse Soleil and Anse a la Mouche on the southwest coast. On the way, take time to stop at the small art galleries clustered around Baie Lazare and Anse aux Pigeons Bleues. Wherever you go, you're bound to find a beach to call your very own.

Two weeks or longer
Inner Islands

Using Mahé, Praslin or La Digue as your base, you have the entire archipelago to choose from. The logistics of travel for such a wide area are best arranged through a good tour operator, such as **Masons Travel** (*Tel: 288 888*), which can organise flights and ferries. Regular ferries make the one-hour voyage from Mahé to Praslin, famed for Vallée de Mai, a UNESCO World Heritage Site and home to the unique *coco de mer*. Praslin, with its lovely beaches, is also the departure point for day trips to Cousin, Curieuse, and Aride Special Nature Reserve. Landing on Aride can be difficult and dangerous, and depends very much on weather conditions.

A twice-daily ferry from Praslin connects with La Digue. On La Digue, walk, cycle or rent a traditional ox-cart to take in the wonders of Anse Source d'Argent, with its sculptured granite boulders and sugar-white sands, the outdoor museum and copra-producing plantation of L'Union Estate, and the rugged beauty of Grande Anse beach in the south.

Outer Islands

Desroches and Alphonse Islands in the Amirantes group are must-sees, not only for their remoteness but for great diving and fishing opportunities. Small aircraft from Mahé make the one-hour journey of a lifetime, flying over ludicrously large turquoise lagoons dotted with scores of perfectly round and misshapen islands, and fringed by blindingly white sands.

Finally, for a journey into a world untouched by humans, Aldabra Atoll, nearer to Madagascar than Mahé, is the Seychelles' equivalent of the 'see Rome and die' experience. This is the ultimate paradise for 150,000 roaming giant land tortoises, unique marine-, bird- and wildlife. Only a few visitors make it there since accommodation is usually reserved for scientists. Although not impossible to reach, it's no secret that you need lots of time and money to visit Aldabra. If you plan to go there, make your arrangements before you arrive in the Seychelles. Cruise ships occasionally anchor off its shores, but it's best to charter a boat from Mahé for the ten-day round trip.

The flag of the Seychelles in the wind

Mahé

Mahé is an island of superlatives so often overlooked by travellers arriving at the international airport. It's the biggest, the most mountainous and the most populated of all the islands in the Seychelles archipelago, yet its capital, Victoria, ranks as one of the smallest in the world. Mahé is also the springboard for reaching the Inner Islands lying to the north by air or sea. These include Praslin, La Digue, Curieuse, Cousin, Cousine, Félicité, Frégate, Silhouette, North and the coral islands of Denis and Bird.

A changing landscape

Some 70,000 people, out of a total population of 81,000 in the Seychelles, live on Mahé, mostly concentrated on the north and east coasts or in Victoria itself. Two-thirds of the capital is built on reclaimed land, which includes a major shipping port and extends southwards all the way to the airport. Land reclamation on the east coast started in the 1970s and is set to continue to cope with increasing housing demands. In 2006, construction began on a man-made island called Eden, a luxurious residential complex, complete with moorings for affluent foreigners who are offered residency as part of the package.

Hidden coves and beaches

For all the development on Mahé, the island is still fairly laid-back, yet when compared with the other Inner Islands there's far more to see and do. Driving or exploring by bus can easily be done in a day, since Mahé is just 27km (17 miles) long and 8km (5 miles) at its widest point. There are 70 beaches for topping up that tan, from the powder-soft sands of Beau Vallon and hidden coves and bays in the west to the surf-beaten granite cliffs of the deep south; walking trails in the verdant Morne Seychellois National Park; excursions to three national marine parks; and Victoria for its Botanical Gardens, a busy little market, and its curious blend of colonial and modern architecture.

Mahé

Anse Major in northern Mahé

VICTORIA – THE PINT-SIZED CAPITAL

Situated on the northeast coast of Mahé and backed by the mountains of Morne Seychellois and Trois Frères, the capital of Victoria is spread around a large bay sheltered by the islands of Sainte Anne, Moyenne, Cerf, Ronde and Longue. In 1778, Mahé was founded by the French and started life as a military post simply known as L'Etablissement, only to remain a forgotten colonial backwater until 1841 when it was named after Queen Victoria.

Such a grand name made little difference to the pace of life, and throughout the British era Victoria remained sparsely populated and largely neglected. Today, things are different,

with 23,300 people living in what is one of the world's tiniest capitals.

Architecturally speaking, the old town at the foot of the mountains is a quirky blend of the old Wild West, with narrow streets and general stores tucked beneath former warehouses, and a provincial Victorian town, with only one set of traffic lights. Modern Victoria is striving to keep up with the 21st century with its new buildings, smart tree-lined pavements and abstract monuments, so you're not likely to fall into a yawning gulley, and there are one or two pleasant restaurants in which to pass the time of day.

Victoria is the only place on Mahé to book ferry and flight tickets, and the tourist office (*Independence Avenue.*

Victoria seen from the sea

The Clock Tower in bustling Victoria

Tel: 610 800) can help with accommodation. The major tour operators have their offices in town. The centre tends to get crowded with traffic so avoid travelling between 8am and 10am and 4pm to 5pm. You can take in the main sights in half a day, preferably the morning when it's a little cooler.

Botanical Gardens

In 1901, a Mauritian botanist, Paul Evenor Rivaltz Dupont, brought species from all over the world to plant in these gardens. A pleasant hour can be spent strolling along pathways bounded by neat lawns and shaded by fruit trees, spice plants, palms and flowering shrubs, finishing with a drink in the cafeteria. An information office at the entrance provides a leaflet describing the botanical beauties on show.

Pride of place goes to the erotic-shaped *coco de mer* palm, of which there are both male and female species. They are only grown here and in Praslin's prolific Vallée de Mai, with a few specimens on Curieuse Island – nowhere else in the world cultivates them. Some unpolished nuts can be bought from the information office, but expect to pay around SR1,500. The gardens also contain six endemic palms.

Just beyond the *coco de mer* palm, and sure to please the kids, is a pen containing giant tortoises, some believed to be over 100 years old, happily mating or munching to pass the time of day. Local kids jump over a

A cannonball flower at the Botanical Gardens

low wall of the pen to ride piggy-back on these gentle creatures, stirring them into action with a rub of the hand on their shells. During November to April, you may see fruit bats that come to feed on mangoes, but more permanent residents such as the tiny endemic fish known as *gouzon*, myriad insects and frogs frequent the freshwater ponds as well as lizards that scuttle in the trees.

Other flora to look out for are double-headed bougainvillea; an abundance of orchids in the orchid house; the cannonball tree whose flowers reveal an explosive riot of cream and red; and the Araucaria tree or drumstick tree from Asia. The drumstick tree seed produces a long stalk crowned with a ball of anthers. Locally known as *tiboko*, many a Seychellois adult can recall being admonished by their elders who would use the drumstick to rap them across the knuckles.

A poignant reminder of the fragility of the environment is evident in an unobtrusive structure hidden beneath trees. Known as the Time Capsule, it contains pledges made by schoolchildren in 1994 to protect the environment for future generations. The Time Capsule will be opened on 3 June 2044, and the hope is that those pledges will have come to fruition. *Mont Fleuri Botanical Garden, Mont Fleuri Road. Tel: 670 500. Open: 8am–5pm. Admission charge.*

National History Museum

If you visit only one of the two museums in Victoria, make it this one. Housed inside the imposing National Library building, the most important exhibit is the Possession Stone laid by the French under Captain Corneille Nicolas Morphy when they claimed the Seychelles in 1756. Other displays include the oldest map of the Seychelles drawn by Portuguese mariner, Pedro Reinel, in 1517; the world's smallest statuette of Queen Victoria; traditional costumes; musical instruments; items salvaged from shipwrecks; and sections on slavery and *gris gris* (black magic), the latter of which is practised by some Seychellois even today.

National Library, Francis Rachel Street. Tel: 321 333. Open: Mon, Tue, Thur & Fri 8.30am–4.30pm, Sat 9am–1pm. Admission charge.

Natural History Museum

Flanking the entrance to this museum are a life-size cement Nile Crocodile, a reminder of times past when the swamps around Mahé were infested with this human-eater, and a dugong, or sea cow, an almost extinct species last seen around Aldabra in 2002. Exhibits include crocodile skulls, displays of endemic birds, stuffed models of hawksbill and green turtles, and a collection of moths and butterflies. There's also an interactive kiosk where you can listen to the bird calls of various species. On the upper floor are prints of tropical plants and scenes of local life by Victorian artist

Look out for the **Unity Monument**, erected in 1986, a futuristic white fish-shaped sculpture symbolising the four pillars of industry on which the Seychelles economy is based: tourism, fishing, agriculture and small industries. Opposite the Marine Charter Association on the waterfront is the **Zomn Libre**, a small figure of an iron man with his arms outstretched. It symbolises the free man and was erected following the coup in 1977, just one year after independence from Britain.

Marianne North, who travelled to the Seychelles in the late 1800s. The originals are at Kew Gardens in London.

Independence Avenue. Tel: 321 333. Open: Mon, Tue, Thur & Fri 8.30am–4.30pm, Sat 9am–1pm. Admission charge.

Mahé

The Unity Monument

Walk: Victoria

This walk covers the main sights. You can park in the free Stadium car park behind the Pirates Arms off Independence Avenue. The main bus terminus is in Palm Street.

Allow 1 hour for a leisurely stroll over a distance of 1km (⅔ mile).

1 The Clock Tower

The heart of town is the Clock Tower, locally known as *lorloz* (clock), a miniature silver version of the clock tower outside London's Victoria Station. Erected in 1903 as a memorial to Queen Victoria, it also commemorates the year when the Seychelles was declared a Crown Colony.

Walk up Independence Avenue, passing the Natural History Museum on the left, to the roundabout to reach the Monument to the Seychellois.

2 Bicentennial Monument

This impressive white sculpture by the Italian artist, Lorenzo Appiani, is also called Trwa Zwazo (three birds). It represents the three continents of

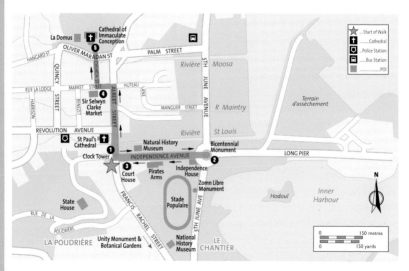

Trwa Zwazo Monument

Africa, Europe and Asia from which the Seychellois people originate. Erected in 1978, the sculpture commemorates 200 years of human occupation.

Cross Independence Avenue and retrace your steps to the Clock Tower to reach the Court House, stopping for a drink at the popular Pirates Arms.

3 Court House

The Court House, dating back to the early 1900s, is a fine example of Victorian architecture. In the gardens is a tiny statue of Queen Victoria perched above a water fountain. The statue is a replica, and the original, in the National History Museum, was unveiled in 1900 to mark Queen Victoria's 60th year on the throne. Beside the Court House is a bust of Pierre Poivre, the French Intendant of Mauritius who was responsible for establishing the Jardin du Roi (*see p38*).

Turn right at the Clock Tower and walk up Albert Street. Take the second road on the left, Market Street, to reach Sir Selwyn Clarke Market.

4 Sir Selwyn Clarke Market

You'll find plenty of local fruit and vegetables, neatly laid-out herbs and spices, and huge stocks of freshly caught fish among the produce in this colourful covered market. The busiest times are Saturday mornings when islanders converge to seek out the best bargains. A few craft shops on the upper floor sell beachwear, *pareos* (sarongs) and unusual coconut souvenirs.

Leave the market by the Market Street exit and walk up Church Street to the Cathedral of the Immaculate Conception in Oliver Maradan Street.

5 Cathedral of Immaculate Conception

The cathedral was completed in 1874 for the Catholic community when the island was under British rule. It has all the hallmarks of French colonial-style architecture, with bold columns and arches, and on Sundays it erupts into life when islanders turn up for Mass. Behind it is a clock that chimes twice on the hour. Some Seychellois wryly remark that it was set that way to ensure that the resident Capuchin monks would have ample time to sober up after heavy drinking binges the night before. To the left of the cathedral is the imposing La Domus (The Domicile), built in 1933 for the Swiss Capuchin order, now used as a seminary for priests.

To reach the bus terminus, walk east along Oliver Maradan Street and continue into Palm Street or take a taxi back to your hotel.

Tuna fishing

Tuna fishing is big business in the Seychelles. The Fishing Port in Mahé's capital, Victoria, is home to the most important tuna landing station and transhipment area in the entire southwestern Indian Ocean and to the world's second-largest cannery.

In 1978, the Seychelles government declared a 320km (200-mile) Exclusive Economic Zone (EEZ), encompassing an area of 1,000,000sq km (386,100 sq miles), to protect its resources from foreign fleets. Part of this area encroached on neighbouring Mauritius' traditional fishing grounds, and the two countries work in unison to coordinate their fishing regulations.

Selling fish at Sir Selwyn Clarke Market, Victoria

The tuna boom began in the early 1980s when French survey ships confirmed huge tuna stocks in the area. By 1984, there were 48 French and Spanish ships fishing in the EEZ, boosting the economy with licensing fees and transhipment charges and posing a challenge to the already thriving tourism industry. This trend continued into the early 2000s, particularly as more foreign fleets landed their catch at Victoria, where the modern port built on reclaimed land provides sophisticated equipment for handling, freezing, packing and shipping. Today, the country exports 300,000 tonnes of tuna per year.

Multinational companies operate in the Fishing Port, employing 2,400 people, and they are only a part of the long chain that brings Seychelles-fished tuna to European supermarket shelves under the brand names of John West, Princes, Petit Navire and Mareblu.

Traditionally, the Seychellois people live on fish, and lots of it, currently consuming 90kg (198lb) per head per year. Many fishing boats can be chartered from Mahé, and you can watch how various fish destined for the cooking pot, such as trevally,

Tuna fishing boats in Victoria

jobfish and the all-time favourite, sailfish, are expertly caught by drawing bait through the water. Skipjack and yellow fin tuna are the main species caught by international fishing vessels in distant waters, but the Seychellois fisherman has no need to risk life and limb when so many other fish can be caught closer to home. Consequently, there is little domestic call for commercially caught tuna, an activity that so far stays firmly in the domain of the international fishing fleets.

The waters around the Seychelles may be teeming with tuna, but policy makers are aware that they can neither continue to increase the fish catch forever nor allow the number of boats that fish in their waters to grow indefinitely. European Union (EU) regulations came into force in 2010 to combat illegal, unreported and unregulated fishing. Yet foreign fishing vessels still break the rules, running the risk of heavy fines. Increased competition from neighbouring Mauritius, which is developing into a regional seafood hub, will mean that the industry will have to make its port services more cost-effective if the Seychelles are to remain the main tuna port of the Indian Ocean.

SOUTHERN MAHÉ

The south is less mountainous and less populated than the north, with small villages portraying a Seychelles of yesteryear, a couple of tourist attractions and dozens of isolated beaches. The best beaches are in the southwest at Anse Intendance, Anse à la Mouche (*see pp12–13*) and Baie Lazare, where there is also a good selection of hotels.

Anse aux Pins

Anse aux Pins is a busy little village strung along the coast road south of the airport. Being the closest village to Victoria on the east coast, with a main bus station and pleasant beach, it's a popular weekend retreat – locals escape the bustle of town while modest guesthouses and eateries appeal to budget travellers. Just before reaching the village there is an unusual nine-hole golf course in a former coconut plantation. Look out for the imposing blue and white former plantation house of the Creole Institute, a research centre for promoting language and literature, which is a wonderful example of Creole architecture. Just beyond the village is Domaine de Val des Près Craft Village (*see opposite*).

4km (2½ miles) south of the airport on the east coast. Bus: No 1 from Victoria.

The Creole Institute at Anse aux Pins

Plantation house at Domaine de Val des Près

Domaine de Val des Près Craft Village

The entrance leads to the former coconut plantation of St Roche Estate, which originally stretched from the shore all the way up to the mountains. In 1920, Douglas Bailey, an employee of the Cable & Wireless Company, bought the Plantation House and ran the plantation for many years, until his death in 1972. The house, dating back to 1870, has been turned into a museum. You can wander through the rooms where colonial furniture dotted with personal effects suggests that the master and his family have just gone out for a walk.

The old kitchens are at the back of the house where meals are still prepared for visitors eating at the on-site restaurant. Nearby is a replica of the servants' quarters complete with the current occupant, Rosa Moncherry, who used to work on the estate. Rosa has many tales to tell of life on the estate as she sits sewing in her simple house, which is decorated with patchwork rugs and walls papered with magazine pages.

The Craft Village, consisting of a dozen gaily painted Creole chalets in front of the house, is worth visiting to see workers making and selling island crafts such as jewellery, perfume soaps, bags and baskets using local materials. A distillery also produces essential oils from cinnamon, eucalyptus, patchouli and lemon grass.

Domaine de Val des Près. Tel: 376 100. Open: 9.30am–5.30pm. Admission charge. Bus: No 1 stops near the entrance.

Anse Royale

Known as Anse Royale, or the Royal Bay, because of its proximity to the original site of the Jardin du Roi or King's Garden (*see below*), this bay is lovely for swimming and snorkelling, but avoid venturing out towards the tiny islet of Île Souris to the north where the currents can be quite strong. The village itself is worth stopping at for a taste of slow island life, friendly folk, small shops and the beach-fronted restaurant, **Kaz Kreol** (*Tel: 371 680*), where nobody bats an eyelid if you turn up in your swimming costume.

11km (7 miles) south of Mahé airport on the east coast. Bus: No 6A from Victoria stops in the village.

Jardin du Roi

The Jardin du Roi occupies the site near the original Jardin du Roi, which was planted in 1771 under the supervision of Pierre Poivre, the French Intendant

of Mauritius. The original was destroyed by a soldier who mistakenly believed Mahé was about to be invaded by the British.

Today, a Plantation House built in 1860 dominates the 34ha (85-acre) estate. It has been in the possession of the same family for three generations, and they have cleared the lands and planted fruit trees, coffee and coconuts. The house has been turned into a small museum full of colonial memorabilia.

You can take a one-hour self-guided walk along paths bounded by tropical plants and spice and fruit trees. Look out for blue pigeons, white-tailed tropicbirds and parakeets in full flight over the forested slopes.

Anse Royale. Tel: 371 313. Open: Mon–Sat 10am–5.30pm, Sun noon–3pm. Admission charge. Drive or walk 1km (²/₃ mile) inland from the village.

Baie Lazare

Named after Lazare Picault who claimed the islands for France in 1742, this pretty village has some interesting art studios exhibiting work by local artists Gerard Devoud, Donald Adelaide and Antonio Filippin, and a takeaway shop beside the police station. The beach to the south of the village sits in a curvaceous bay, normally as calm as a mill pond, but wild and windswept during the southeast monsoon when fierce rollers pound ashore.

4km (2¹/₂ miles) south of Anse à la Mouche on the west coast. Bus: No 6A from Victoria.

Welcome to Baie Lazare

Drive: Morne Seychellois National Park

This steep, winding 14km (8¹/₂-mile) drive includes access to optional walking trails inside the national park (see pp49–50).

Allow 1 hour.

From Victoria, follow the signs for Bel Air Road for 150m (165yds) to reach Bel Air Cemetery.

1 Bel Air Cemetery

This cemetery has its origins in the late 18th century. Among the moss-covered headstones are the graves of Jean-François Hodoul, a famous French corsair (*see p59*) who retired in the Seychelles, and Pierre-Louis Poiret, an enigmatic figure who claimed to be the son of Louis XVI. An obelisk marks the grave of a 14-year-old giant who was poisoned and said to be the son of a prominent Seychellois figure.

Turn left outside the cemetery, following the road uphill for 3km (2 miles) to Chemin Sans Souci, watching out for magnificent views of the east coast before reaching the black gates of Sans Souci House.

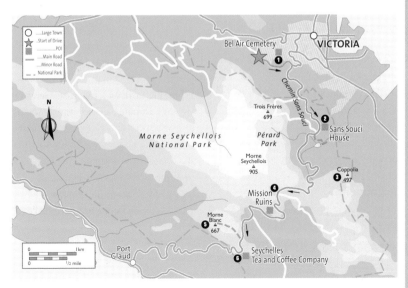

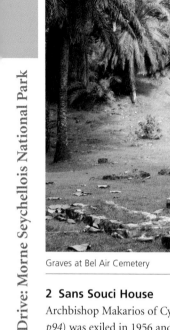

Graves at Bel Air Cemetery

2 Sans Souci House

Archbishop Makarios of Cyprus (*see p94*) was exiled in 1956 and spent a year at this lodge. The house was later used as the American ambassador's residence and is now privately owned. You can share the same views of densely wooded forest and, like the Archbishop, ponder the significance of Sans Souci, which means 'without worry'.

Continue past the driveway for 1.5km (1 mile). A trail indicates Trois Frères on the right and Coppolia on the left. Park beside the Coppolia sign.

3 Coppolia

This is a good place to take in the magical silence of the national park. You may see graceful white tropicbirds or spot endemic birds such as the Seychelles bulbul or blue pigeon. The

walk to the top of Coppolia at 497m (1,630ft) is strenuous but there are splendid views of the east coast. Allow at least two hours for the return trip.

Follow the Chemin Sans Souci for another 2km (1¼ miles) to reach a panoramic viewpoint at Mission Ruins signposted on the right.

4 Mission Ruins

These ruins (*see pp108–9*) date back to 1875 when British missionaries built a school for child slaves. Although slavery was abolished in 1834, the practice continued. British anti-slavery ships rescued thousands of slaves, many of whom were children, and brought them to Mission.

Drive for another 2.5km (1½ miles), looking to your right for the walking trail to Morne Blanc.

5 Morne Blanc

Moss covers the forest rocks and tree trunks in this moist region of lemon grass and tea plantations. The white granite slopes of Morne Blanc at 667m (2,190ft) protrude above the forest canopy as you continue the drive southwards. If you undertake this walk it is only 1km (2/3 mile) but very steep. *Continue for 200m (220yds) to reach the car park of the Seychelles Tea and Coffee Company.*

6 Seychelles Tea and Coffee Company

This working factory produces a small amount of tea blended with imported tea from Sri Lanka for local use and 45 tonnes of organic tea for export. You can buy flavoured tea from The Tea Tavern at the factory.
Tel: 378 221. Open: Mon–Fri 7am–4pm. Guided tours available. Admission charge. The road winds through switchbacks to Port Glaud on the west coast.

Picking the raw ingredients for the Tea and Coffee Company

Drive: Morne Seychellois National Park

NORTHERN MAHÉ

There are three good roads from the capital, Victoria, that cut across the north of Mahé from east to west. The road to Beau Vallon winds uphill, giving views over Victoria, before continuing to Glacis and North Point, and during rush hours it can be slow. Less busy is Chemin Sans Souci, which skirts the Morne Seychellois National Park to emerge at Port Glaud. South of Victoria is La Misère road to Grande Anse, the fastest and most direct route to the southwest coast.

Aside from the irresistible tourist beach of Beau Vallon, there are many opportunities for sunning and snorkelling in bays and rocky coves at Glacis. Rounding the northern part of Mahé, the road clings closely to the shore from North East Pont to Pointe Cèdre with an attractive albeit rocky beach. South from Beau Vallon, the road runs out giving way to steep, sloping rocky hillsides, or *glacis*, and

walking trails passing delightful soft sandy coves lead to two marine parks teeming with marine life. However, the jewel in the crown is the Morne Seychellois National Park (*see pp39–41 & pp49–50*) with three mountain peaks, the highest of which is the grand Morne Seychellois at 905m (2,970ft), surrounded by mist forests and the habitat of unique flora and fauna.

Baie Ternay National Marine Park

Baie Ternay and Port Launay (*see p51*) would be one huge marine park were it not for the headland of Cap Matoopa separating them. Aware that the corals off Mahé's east coast were being adversely affected by silt build-up and land reclamation schemes, the government was keen to preserve those in the west and in 1979 declared them national marine parks.

Baie Ternay nestles between Cap Ternay and Cap Matoopa on the west coast and is only accessible by sea.

A school of yellowtail snappers

The densely wooded coast at Glacis

Apart from yachts seeking shelter from high winds and rough seas during the southeast monsoon, the marine park also lures snorkellers and scuba divers. Here you can explore coral-encrusted wrecks and spot myriad fish darting over huge carpet anemone in waters less than 25m (82ft) deep. If you enjoy night diving, join an organised dive with the **Underwater Centre Seychelles** (*see opposite*) and feast your eyes on an extravaganza of dancing rays while moray eels and lobsters search in crevices for food.

The *Catalina* catamaran also sails to Baie Ternay after picking up footsore walkers from the pre-arranged guided coastal walk from Danzilles to Anse Major (*see p46*). The trip includes a tasty on-board barbecue and great snorkelling. If you want to explore the deserted white beach or hand-feed fish on the way, the *Catalina*'s rubber dinghy will take you ashore.

On west coast and only accessible by sea. Masons Travel (tel: 288 888) offers an exclusive guided walk from Danzilles to Anse Major and pickup by catamaran for a barbecue lunch at Baie Ternay Marine Park.

Underwater Centre Seychelles (next door to the Berjaya Beau Vallon Hotel; tel: 345 445) provides a full range of Professional Association of Diving Instructors (PADI)-approved dive packages and opportunities for visitors to get involved in marine conservation projects that include whale shark monitoring (www.diveseychelles.com.sc).

Beau Vallon

Beau Vallon is Mahé's main tourist beach, lying in a deep bay on the west coast just 5km (3 miles) from the capital, Victoria. Its popularity has increased in recent years, with visitors attracted by more affordable accommodation, thereby saving on the time and expense incurred in getting to Praslin and La Digue as soon as they arrive at the airport.

By European standards, Beau Vallon is a small, low-key resort with just three hotels, a handful of guesthouses, bars and restaurants tucked unobtrusively behind *takamaka* and palm trees. Its

beauty lies in the gently shelving pristine sands, clear waters, and views of Silhouette and North islands on the horizon. If you're staying at one of the accommodations to the south of Beau Vallon, it's a delight to stroll north along the beach towards the 'village' end where friendly fishermen tend their nets and people go about their daily business running small guesthouses and eateries.

You could spend a few days or indeed your entire holiday in Beau Vallon, having great fun getting to know the local people and doing more than soaking up the sun. Most activity

Banana boat ride in Beau Vallon bay

centres on the Coral Strand Hotel where, on the slip road behind the beach, you'll find boat hire, dive centres and fishing operators politely touting for business, plus a few restaurants and bars to while away the evenings. The beach is safe for children and there's even a lifeguard on duty. Water activity includes windsurfing, banana boat rides, parasailing and glass-bottom boat excursions to Port Launay and Baie Ternay National Marine Parks.

5km (3 miles) west from Victoria along the winding Beau Vallon road. The best operator for diving and snorkelling trips and excursions to Silhouette is Big Blue Divers (Tel: 261 106). For glass-bottom boat trips contact Teddy at Northern Charter Sales Office, Mare Anglaise (Tel: 511 198).

Sun, sea and sand at Beau Vallon

Bel Ombre

Bel Ombre, a tiny resort at the south corner of Beau Vallon beach, has just one hotel, the luxurious Fisherman's Cove. Noted for its fine snorkelling around the rocks, its pleasant coastal walks and a few upmarket restaurants conspire to entice self-catering visitors to attractive bungalows and cottages scattered along gentle hillsides.

The tourist office (*opposite the Fisherman's Cove Hotel*) can provide you with maps and information on Mahé generally. Not much happens at Bel Ombre, but the area is noted for a famous treasure hunt carried out by Reginald Cruise Wilkins, a Grenadier Guard, who in 1949 happened to be in Mahé recovering from malaria. Wilkins spent a lifetime unravelling cryptograms of buried treasure left by 18th-century pirate Olivier Le Vasseur (*see p58*) and was convinced that it was hidden at Bel Ombre. In the 1970s, Bel Ombre woke from its lethargy when Wilkins brought in equipment in an attempt to find the treasure. He died in 1977 and his sons took up the hunt. Even though nothing has been found, the area continues to excite amateur treasure seekers who dream that the fabulous treasure, today valued at $US160 million, is buried somewhere in Bel Ombre.

2km (1¼ miles) west of Beau Vallon on the west coast. Bus: No 21 from Victoria stops near the Fisherman's Cove Hotel.

The Seychelles vanilla

Danzilles to Anse Major

During the 19th century, a coastal path was built to link the hamlet of Danzilles with the beautiful beach of Anse Major. The path takes in the coastal region of the Morne Seychellois National Park and, although gentle to start with as you pass by pretty houses with gardens bursting with tropical flowers and fruit trees, it is not for the faint-hearted. You should carry water and wear trainers as there is some serious scrambling across large expanses of boulders and granite rock formations, or *glacis*. It is certainly worth the effort to get there, if only for the views of Silhouette and North Islands and a viewpoint over the glittering turquoise bay of Anse Major.

Endemic plants to look out for are the Latanier millepatte palm (*Nephrosperma vanhoutteana*), the Vacoa marron screwpine (*Pandanus sechellarum*) and the leafless fleshy green stems of the Seychelles vanilla (*Vanilla phalaenopsis*) draped across bushes and trees. You may also spot the Seychelles blue pigeon but are more likely to hear the chatter of the Indian mynah bird and cooing doves. Allow at least two hours for the return trip and be prepared for some rocky inclines. If you want to be picked up by catamaran, you should contact Masons Travel (*see p151*) who can pick you up in the *Catalina* when it calls at Anse Major.

Anse Major is a breathtakingly beautiful sandy bay backed by verdant mountains, and is as isolated today as it was in the past when it was a private estate owned by a wealthy childless French widow. She apparently disapproved of her sister running off with a Seychellois, and to punish her left the land to a Roman Catholic Mission. Workers on the estate, now long abandoned, used to produce essential oil from patchouli, the strongly scented mint-like shrubs used for perfumery, and cultivate vanilla, cinnamon and citrus fruits before loading the produce into pirogues for shipping to Victoria. You can still see some of the trees in the pathways behind the beach.

Bus: No 21 leaves Victoria for Danzilles on the west coast. Anse Major is 2.4km (1½ miles) southwest of Danzilles.

Grande Anse

The isolated beach of Grande Anse, with its granite boulders and huge sweep of white sands, is best reserved for sunbathing since treacherous currents have caught strong swimmers unaware. Beyond the headland to the south, the family-oriented Meridien Barbarons Hotel (*see p149*) dominates Barbarons Bay, but even here you should take note of warning flags, especially during the southeast monsoon from May to September.

The Barbarons Estate, a short drive south of the hotel, used to be the biggest coconut plantation in Mahé. Nowadays, the coastal views are marred by the masts of the Indian Ocean Relay Station, which provides satellite links with the BBC World Service. Inland, trees march uphill towards the winding La Misère road where, between 1966 and 1996, the Americans had their own satellite tracking station. When they left, many Seychellois had married officers and technicians and emigrated to America. Little remains of the original site apart from the clubhouse, now used as the Seychelles Tourism Academy. The area is set to change with the construction of a six-storey palace for Sheikh Khalifa of Abu Dhabi. *Take the Misère Road from Victoria to Grande Anse. Turn right and continue for 500m (550yds) to reach Grande Anse Beach.*

The dramatic Grande Anse beach

Labrin Market

This is the only market in the Seychelles, and it opens at 4pm. It started out in 2005 as an experiment to encourage interaction between tourists and locals and has become something of a tradition. Islanders from all over Mahé gather on the slip road behind Beau Vallon beach and set up stalls to sell local produce, souvenirs made from coconut and wood, tasty Creole snacks, and drinks and beachwear. Some of the alfresco catering equipment is quite sophisticated with shiny modern gas burners and stoves. You'll also find huge ice-boxes containing the day's catch waiting to be cooked to order beside rickety barbecues, with the aroma stimulating your appetite for the evening meal at nearby restaurants. The atmosphere is friendly and laid-back, with families and tourists tucking into crispy fried breadfruit chips, spicy local sausages, barbecued *job* (snapper), sizzling fried tuna or *karang* (trevally), and all of it eaten on the hoof. Try the mango drinks and the local *fisiter*, a refreshing non-alcoholic drink produced from the fruit of the golden apple tree and also used to make chutney. Sometimes impromptu Creole bands play music beneath the trees.

5km (3 miles) west from Victoria. Wed and last Sat of the month 4–9pm. Bus: Nos 20, 22 and 24 from Victoria stop on the slip road running parallel with Beau Vallon beach, 100m (110yds) from the Coral Strand Hotel.

Stock up on some souvenirs at Labrin Market

Waterfall in Morne Seychellois National Park

Morne Seychellois National Park

This national park was created in 1979. It covers a huge area of 3,045ha (7,500 acres), or 20 per cent of the area of Mahé, and is 10km (6 miles) long and between 2km and 3km (1¼ and 1¾ miles) across. It is the habitat of many endemic plants and animals, and the Morne Seychellois mountain at 905m (2,970ft) and other mountains provide the main water supply to Mahé's expanding population.

Hikers may enjoy a series of walking trails of varying difficulty, exploring the park's magnificent diversity from low coastal forest to drier palm forests and the more inaccessible humid mist forests on the heights. The rewards are great, if only to listen to the chatter of birds like the bulbul and see the flitting movements of tiny endemic frogs, no bigger than a human fingernail, and the furtive tiger chameleon looking as though it's been dabbed with a yellow paintbrush, or fruit bats roosting in the trees. The trails are well marked and leaflets describing them are available from the Botanical Gardens in Victoria, which can also provide details of qualified guides.

Some of these trails should only be undertaken with a guide. One of the best guides is Basil Beaudouin (*Tel: 241 790*) who has been leading tours for 17 years and meets clients at the Coral Strand Hotel (*every Monday at 6pm*). He knows the trails intimately, having grown up in the forests, and he'll show you unique species of flora and fauna, like the strange carnivorous pitcher

The beach at Port Glaud

plant (*Nepenthes pervillei*), which feeds on insects, and the oddly named jellyfish tree (*Medusagyne oppositifolia*), unique to the Seychelles.

Take Chemin Sans Souci, a good winding road south from Victoria, which skirts the park and emerges at Port Glaud on the west coast. Bus: No 14 from Victoria also covers this route, stopping at convenient points near the walking trails.

Port Glaud

Port Glaud sits in a gentle bay facing the large, privately owned island of Thérèse and one of the smallest granitic islands in the region, L'Islette. The area underwent upgrading with the 2010 opening of the Constance Ephelia Hotel dominating Port Launay Marine Park.

Nearby is a huge expanse of wetlands supporting seven species of mangrove in the region. Port Glaud waterfall provides some inland distraction. The waterfall, best seen after heavy rains, tumbles from the cliffs of the 667m (2,190ft) high Morne Blanc into rivulets and streams and is the source of Mahé's main water supply. Entrance to the falls is by fee to a local family who live in a house beside the car park. This fee goes towards maintaining the paths and timber stairway that follow the contours of a steep-sided gorge. You will have to negotiate some slippery boulders at the bottom to get the best views unless you are content to listen to the gushing sounds of the cascading waters. On the way, look out for endemic plants like the thief palm

lining the banks, and freshwater prawns, shrimps and crabs foraging in rock pools.

5km (3 miles) northwest from Grande Anse. To reach the waterfalls, take the path immediately after the church at Port Glaud and follow the sign marked 'Waterfalls'. After 1.5km (1 mile) there is a small car park. It takes about five minutes by foot to reach the falls. Admission charge.

Port Launay National Marine Park

Port Launay National Marine Park, sandwiched between Cap Matoopa and La Plaine, is really an extension of Baie Ternay. It is the only marine park that is accessible by road, so if you want to avoid the crowds it's best to go mid-week. Sheltered by the islands of Conception and Thérèse, it is blessed with a long, curvaceous beach with *takamaka* trees providing plenty of shade, and it's a perfect spot for a picnic. The main attractions are swimming and snorkelling, and many boats drop anchor here, depositing passengers to explore the reef. The area is also renowned for sightings of the protected whale shark that calls by to feed in the plankton-rich waters during August and from October to January.

20km (12 miles) from Victoria on the west coast. Bus: 9, 13 and 14 from Victoria regularly ply the route, but make sure you leave enough time for the last bus at around 4.30pm.

Explore the reef at Port Launay National Marine Park

Sainte Anne National Marine Park

Declared a national marine park in 1973, the first in the Indian Ocean, this area just off the east coast of Victoria consists of five islands – Île au Cerf, Longue, Moyenne, Ronde and Sainte Anne. Although the corals have lost much of their sparkle due to the effects of El Niño in the late 1990s and silt build-up from reclamation projects, there is still an amazing variety of marine life.

Tour operators offer snorkelling and glass-bottom boat trips or excursions in a semi-submersible, which may include lunch on Île au Cerf, Moyenne or Ronde islands. Alternatively, you can book a trip independently at the **Marine Charter Association** in Victoria. Whichever way you go, there are panoramic views of the mountains of Mahé.

An aerial view of the five islands

Cerf Island Marine Park Resort

Marine Charter Association, Victoria Harbour. Tel: 322 126. Open: 8am–noon & 1–4pm. Admission charge for marine park area.

Île au Cerf (Cerf Island)

This low-lying, densely wooded island is just 1.7km (1 mile) long and barely 0.9km (¹/₂ mile) across. There are no shops or roads for the 80 or so islanders who live here – only beautiful beaches bookended by smooth granite boulders. The island attracts locals and tourists seeking an affordable getaway from the traffic of Mahé.

Boats from Mahé land on the beach on the south coast and you wade ashore; here the bar of L'Habitation Cerf Island Hotel provides drinks and snacks. If you stay the night, there are three accommodations, and reservations are essential – the simple plantation house-style L'Habitation Cerf Island Hotel, which has ten rooms and chalets; the intimate chalets of Cerf Island Resort with grand ocean views from the restaurant, which is preferred by honeymooners (*see p82*), and Villa de Cerfs with four rooms. Guests can swim, snorkel or take a pedalo to reach the other islands.

It is worth exploring a trail that cuts across Cerf Island, starting from L'Habitation Cerf Island Hotel in the south and ending on the north coast where there is a delightful beach with lounging palm trees providing shade over white sands. Allow a couple of hours, preferably in the cool of the morning, to complete the trek. Pass behind houses until you reach a narrow jungly trail, and stop to take in the sound of birdsong and soft breezes wafting through the eerie silence. At the summit of the trail, look out for the tangled bushes of the coco plum, planted in the early 20th century all over the islands as an anti-erosion measure. It bears an edible but tasteless fruit, but the bushes have become so invasive that they smother other vegetation. The path then descends, revealing resplendent views of the neighbouring islands of Sainte Anne, Moyenne, Ronde and Longue.

15 minutes by boat from Victoria Harbour or by helicopter. Neighbouring islands can also arrange transport to Cerf.

Longue

Longue (Long Island) used to be a prison until inmates were moved to Mahé in 2007. By late 2011, this 9ha (22-acre) rock, for so long off-limits to the public, will be transformed into the exclusive Shangri-La Resort, complete with restaurants, spa and wedding chapel with 360° ocean views.

15 minutes by boat from Victoria Harbour or by helicopter.
www.shangri-la.com

The turquoise waters of Sainte Anne National Marine Park

There are over 100 tortoises on Moyenne

Moyenne

The 9ha (22-acre) island of Moyenne was bought in 1962 by former British newspaper editor Brendon Grimshaw who fulfilled a dream of living on an island home with gardens bursting with native flora and views across to Mahé. It is the most interesting of all the islands to visit thanks to Grimshaw, an inveterate animal lover who enjoys receiving visitors and has become something of a celebrity and legendary storyteller.

If you go at low tide, you feel like a castaway washed ashore as you wade through shallow clear waters to clamber on to a blindingly white sand spit. The Jolly Roger Bar and Restaurant on the island provides an excellent Creole buffet lunch amid a natural setting of palms and cooing birds with occasional appearances by Derek, a septuagenerian tortoise, one of 102 owned by Brendon Grimshaw.

There are rumours of buried pirate treasure on the island, and tales of ghosts, including that of a canine-crazy Brit, Emma Best, who had a house built here for a pack of stray dogs in the early 1900s. You can walk past the ruins of the house along a path planted with endemic species. The path has been specially widened to accommodate Grimshaw's growing population of happy roaming tortoises and a menagerie of friendly dogs and cats.

When Grimshaw bought Moyenne, he found it sparse, harsh and barely habitable, and his fascinating story is told in his book, *A Grain of Sand*, available in Mahé's bookshops or from the author himself. Over the years,

Sainte Anne and the other islands seen from Victoria

Grimshaw has transformed Moyenne into a bountiful island bursting with flora and fauna, and he aims to keep it as an environmental treasure trove for all those who step ashore.

15 minutes by boat from Victoria Harbour; book through Creole Travel Services (Tel: 297 001), which runs exclusive tours and lunch at the Jolly Roger Restaurant.

Ronde

The tiny 12ha (5-acre) Round Island used to be a quarantine station for female sufferers of leprosy. In 2010 it was transformed into a haven of luxury dominated by one hotel – Round Island Resort.

The island is 26m (85ft) above sea level and is clothed in a mantle of tropical vegetation. It's small enough to walk around in less than 20 minutes and has several beaches and coves. With only ten chalets, inspired by local Creole architecture, nestling on the perimeter of the island and hidden by dense foliage, a stay here guarantees total seclusion and a feeling of going back to a time when Seychelles was virtually uninhabited.

Yet old traditions blend seamlessly with new technology on this island retreat. Broadband and satellite TV in the spacious chalets complement a private swimming pool, outdoor decking and direct access to sparkling coves.

10 minutes by boat from Victoria Harbour. www.enchantedseychelles.com

Sainte Anne

In 1770, the first French settlers lived on Sainte Anne, the largest of the islands in the marine park. In 1832, a whaling station was established in the south although there is little evidence of this today. During the British colonial period, the island was better known for its prolific coconut plantation, and during World War II it was used as a fuel store.

Today, the island is the domain of the luxurious Sainte Anne Resort, and casual visits by day-trippers are discouraged. If you are not staying at the resort, you can book lunch at the rather expensive restaurant and arrive by the hotel's private ferry or alternatively charter a boat. For guests staying here, free boat rides are provided to the mainland.

Sainte Anne remains an important nesting ground for hawksbill turtles that come ashore to lay their eggs. It is a beautiful island, featuring a peak of 250m (820ft) rising above thick tropical vegetation and skirted by white beaches, notably Anse Cabot in the north and Anse Cimetière in the south.

15 minutes by boat from Victoria Harbour or by helicopter.

Sainte Anne island

Pirates of the Seychelles

'Find my treasure who can!' were the last words croaked by Olivier Le Vasseur in 1730 as he stood on the gallows in the town of Saint Paul in Bourbon (Réunion island) and tossed a sheaf of paper to the baying crowd. The papers contained details of where to find one of the most fabulous pirates' treasure troves ever plundered in the Indian Ocean. Many people have tried to find the treasure and failed, but serious treasure hunters agree that the most likely spot is at Bel Ombre on Mahé's west coast. The most determined was an ex-British

The Bel Air grave of Jean-François Hodoul

grenadier named Reginald Cruise-Wilkins who spent a lifetime dredging the coastline only to unearth a few coins and trinkets before he died in 1977.

The list of pirates, corsairs and ne'er-do-wells in the Caribbean reads, in seafaring terms, like a cast of nautical film stars. In the 16th and 17th centuries, life for a pirate in the Caribbean had become difficult due to heavy policing. Old cut-throats, such as Henry Avery, Edward England, Thomas Tew and Bartholomew Roberts, had run east and were finding rich pickings from merchant ships from Europe, plying their trade with the East Indies in the Indian Ocean. By the 1670s, the whole Indian Ocean littoral, from the Red Sea to the southwestern shores of the Indian subcontinent, was infested with pirates. Some 1,500 were based on Saint Mary's island off Madagascar where a pirates' republic called Libertalia was established.

Following growing rivalry between the French and British for supremacy of the lucrative Indian Ocean route, not all new buccaneers on the block were strictly pirates but privateers or corsairs armed with a letter of

Praslin's Côte d'Or, or 'Gold Coast'

marque. This document issued by the French authorities gave them carte blanche to raid any vessel in the name of France. The Seychelles was a favourite place for passing ships to stop and careen and to restock with supplies, and the islands gave many a pirate vessel good cover from which to ambush them.

Jean-François Hodoul was the Seychelles' most successful corsair. After years at sea, he knew the islands better than anyone and, attracted by the prospect of earning a good income, fitted the profile perfectly, notching up many successful attacks on British shipping and handing a good portion of the pickings to the French. He eventually retired and settled in his native Mahé and became well respected as a justice of the peace. Unusually for a man of his trade he died peacefully, and his gravestone can still be seen in the upper section of the Bel Air cemetery.

Today, you still come across names of places associated with pirates. In Mahé, there is the secluded Anse Forbans, which means 'Pirates' Bay', and a rocky islet in the harbour at Victoria is named after Hodoul who is said to have used Silhouette Island as a hideout, secreting his plunder in the lush tropical grounds. On Praslin, there is Côte d'Or, which means 'Gold Coast', and both Frégate and Moyenne islands, former pirates' lairs, bristle with rumours of buried treasure and ghosts.

Praslin and satellite islands

Blessed with beautiful beaches and devoid of towns, it's little wonder that Praslin, with a population of 7,000, just 45km (28 miles) from Mahé, appeals to those seeking the comfortable desert island experience. Most make the 15-minute flip from Mahé, landing at the airstrip on the west coast, while others are content to sprout sea legs for the hour-long voyage aboard the Cat Cocos *catamaran from the Inter Island quay in Victoria, landing at Baie Sainte Anne in the southeast.*

Whether you arrive by air or sea, you soon realise that this island, the second largest of the Inner Islands group, is less mountainous, less populated and even more laid-back than Mahé. Most islanders are employed in fishing,

agriculture and tourism or commute to Praslin on business.

There is a good choice of accommodation to suit all budgets, some splendid eateries, and driving along a good network of roads is quite

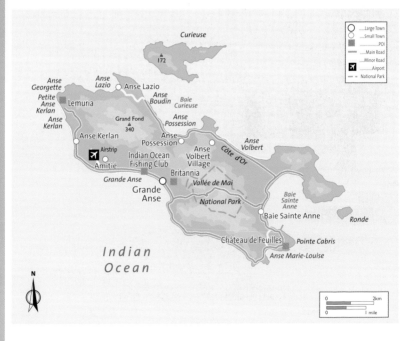

sedate. However, for the full local experience, opt for the irregular bone-shaking buses, sharing your seat with tiny tots and cheerful grannies.

Praslin's premier attractions are the Vallée de Mai, with its unique primeval forests of the *coco de mer* palm, and stunning Anse Lazio beach in the north. You can also island-hop to Curieuse, Cousin and Aride, a trio of islands appealing to nature lovers.

Beautiful Anse Lazio beach

62

Coco de mer

It takes ten years to ripen and it has a fleshy, fibrous casing. The jelly-like contents are said to be a delicacy. It weighs up to 23kg (50lb) and looks like a rounded pair of female thighs complete with tufts of pubic hair.

Female *coco de mer* palm in the Botanical Gardens, Victoria

In 1881, General Gordon referred to it as the 'forbidden fruit' when he visited the Seychelles, and in 2001, a London sex emporium run by Sam Roddick, daughter of Anita Roddick of Body Shop fame, was named after it.

It's called the *coco de mer*. This erotic-shaped nut, which grows only on two of the 115 islands in the Seychelles, is so valuable and coveted that it's become a collectors' item, fetching prices of up to $US900.

Nobody knows where the *coco de mer* came from, but dozens of myths are associated with it. Some wrongly believe it originated from the Maldives, hence the scientific name, *Lodoicea maldivica*, others that it grew in a magic garden at the bottom of the sea, while folklore maintains certain death for those foolish enough to witness what is believed to be the midnight mating ritual between the male and female palm.

Sailors found the nuts floating in the Indian Ocean long before the palms were discovered growing naturally in 1768 in the deeply wooded Vallée de Mai on Praslin, now a UNESCO World Heritage Site. Many nuts were brought to Europe in the 16th century where they ended up as

A polished *coco de mer*

---

that the palms can probably live for between 200 and 400 years.

The *coco de mer* used to thrive on the islands of Saint Pierre, Chauve-Souris and Ronde, where people would use the fronds to make thatched roofs and turn the husks into utensils for domestic use or carve out souvenirs for tourists. Now, it is found only on Praslin (with a few palms on Curieuse), but you can see a mature female palm, planted in 1956 by the Duke of Edinburgh, in the Botanical Gardens in Mahé.

The Ministry of the Environment strictly controls the collection of this rare protected species, and poaching has become a problem. You can buy a nut from the **Seychelles Islands Foundation** in Mahé, which manages the Vallée de Mai on behalf of the Seychelles government. Money collected from sales and entrance fees to the Vallée de Mai goes towards conservation management projects. Expect to pay upwards of SR1,500 for an unpolished nut and considerably more if it has been polished and varnished, but you'll be safe in the knowledge that it is a genuine *coco de mer*, sold with an export permit. *Seychelles Islands Foundation. La Ciotat Building, Mont Fleuri, Victoria, Mahé. Tel: 321 735. www.sif.sc. Open: Mon–Fri 9am–5pm.*

objets d'art in the private galleries of the aristocracy.

Male palms grow to about 30m (100ft) high and the females to 24m (80ft) high. The female appears heavily pregnant, with up to a dozen nuts clamped to the upper reaches of her trunk, while the male, with its broad fan-shaped leaves and drooping phallic-like 1m (3ft) long catkins, is believed to provide shade and protection and facilitate wind pollination. Scientific studies show

Walk: Vallée de Mai

Vallée de Mai, an area of 19.5ha (48 acres) in the east of Praslin, was declared a UNESCO World Heritage Site in 1984 for its unique dense jungles of the coco de mer *palm (see pp62–3) and other endemic flora.*

This walk covers 1km (⅔ mile) and is best done in the morning when it is cooler.

Allow 1 hour.

1 Entrance

It's a short climb on uneven steps to the entrance where every ticket is checked to ensure that nobody is stranded overnight. The shaded kiosk nearby is a good place to soak up the atmosphere. Note that smoking is strictly prohibited. You may spot endemic birds like the black parrot or a tenrec scurrying across the forest floor.

Open: 8am–5pm. Admission charge.
Bus: No 61 from Baie Sainte Anne, Grande Anse and Côte d'Or stops right outside the Visitor Centre.
If driving, there is a large car park directly opposite.

The path continues uphill to a fingerpost. Take the right fork indicating 'North Trail' to reach the firebreaks and forest edge.

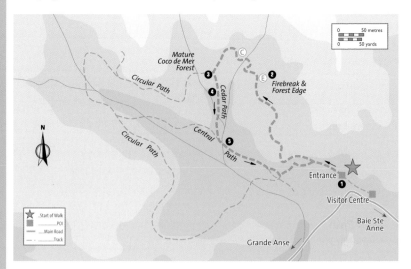

2 Firebreak and forest edge

Here, numerous young *coco de mer* palms sprout from undergrowth on the forest floor. These palms have long leaf stems but no trunk. Marker E indicates a firebreak on your right. This was deliberately created in 1990 following an outbreak of fire, which destroyed many palms. The area is planted with a fire-resistant tree locally known as *Kalis dipap* and other ornamental and fruit trees.

Continue north where the path levels out to the next marker C, passing granite boulders. Listen to the sound of water from hidden streams and, at the next marker post, turn left onto Cedar Path to reach mature forests of coco de mer.

3 Mature *coco de mer* forest

Deep in the primeval forest, you'll find a riot of mature palms. Their mammoth fan-shaped fronds form a dense sylvan canopy obliterating the sky, and the only sound is the clattering of palm leaves as the wind rushes through. Many of the palms are more than 200 years old and thrive in the rich soil provided by nutrients of fallen leaves. Notice the long catkins of the male palms and the massive oval nuts, weighing up to 20kg (44lb), clamped around the upper trunk of the shorter female palms.

Turn left at the next fingerpost, following the pathway marked Cedar Path.

4 Cedar Path

On your right is a stream flowing over gravel beds. This stream and several tributaries converge on a waterfall, 500m (550yds) to the southwest in an area outside the Vallée de Mai, providing water for the west coast. Linger awhile and you may spot freshwater crabs and transparent shrimps in the shallows and dragonflies and damselflies skimming the water for insects.

Continue along Cedar Path and turn left at Central Path.

5 Central Path

On the right of Central Path is a ravine containing a superb collection of pandanus and screwpines. Some palms are swathed in philodendron giving them a jungly appearance, but this is an invasive plant that has to be cut back. Depending on the time of year, you will also see flowering fruit and other ornamental trees and endemic birds such as the sunbird, blue pigeon, black parrot and bulbul.

Continue along Central Path to reach the exit.

Forest, Vallée de Mai

Beaches of Praslin
Anse Kerlan, Petite Anse Kerlan and Anse Georgette

These three beaches hug the northwestern tip of Praslin's coast, and during September to February turtles come ashore to lay their eggs. Anse Kerlan is the longest – a smooth, shelving white beach bookended by smooth boulders and backed by *takamaka* trees. Further north, the luxurious villas of the Lemuria Resort (*see p152*) hide behind Petite Anse Kerlan, a smaller deserted beach at the end of which is the hotel boathouse. From here, take trips along the coast to Anse Georgette.

Lemuria Resort is home to Seychelles' only 18-hole golf course.

Anse Georgette beach

If you're a guest of the hotel, you can stroll beside the golf course, dotted with lakes and streams, following the tracks to Anse Georgette. If the hotel is not full, they will normally let you in, but it's best to telephone first. The walk from the golf course takes about 20 minutes, reaching a plateau where there are views of Cousin and the private island of Cousine. Continue to the 15th hole for gorgeous views of Anse Georgette.

On Praslin's northwest coast 4km (2¼ miles) west from the airport at Grande Anse.

Anse Lazio

This curvaceous bay has all the attributes of a Seychellois beach; talcum powder soft sands, clear blue waters, smooth granitic boulders, windswept palms and *takamaka* trees leaning across the shore provide natural shade. Travel magazines have extolled its virtues, it's a top location for fashion shoots, and in the 1980s scenes from *Castaway*, a film based on Lucy Irvine's book about life on a desert island, were filmed here. Midweek it's a romantic haven for snorkelling, swimming and sunbathing, and there's plenty of parking and two restaurants.

Anse Lazio is 800m (875yds) northwest of Anse Boudin on Praslin's north coast. Buses from Vallée de Mai via Baie Sainte Anne and Côte d'Or terminate at Anse Boudin. It's then a 15-minute hike over the headland to reach the bay, but there are taxis to take you back up again.

Giant boulders on Anse Lazio beach

Anse Marie-Louise

Anse Marie-Louise is the most picturesque of the eight beaches on the south coast from Grande Anse in the west to Baie Sainte Anne in the east, and it's well worth spending some time here lazing on the beach, swimming in the clear waters or just enjoying a picnic. From the main Grande Anse coast road, take the path just before the road rises steeply for the Château de Feuilles Hotel (*see p154*) at Pointe Cabris. The hotel makes a good stop for a drink where you can also enjoy fabulous views of the bay.

On Praslin's south coast, 8km (5 miles) southeast from Grande Anse.

Anse Possession

Anse Possession is a lovely deep bay dotted with small coves and is sheltered by Curieuse Island. In 1768, the French claimed possession of Praslin, celebrating the event with a lead plaque. An English naval officer, so the story goes, is credited with removing the plaque and replacing it with one of his own. Nowadays, it is a tranquil retreat with only a few guesthouses, and a popular weekend picnic spot. To the east of the bay, at Anse Petite Cour, is La Reserve Hotel, totally destroyed in the 2004 tsunami. It was completely rebuilt, and reopened in 2006.

3km (2 miles) northwest of Anse Volbert village on Côte d'Or.

Self-catering villas at Côte d'Or

Baie Sainte Anne

This little fishing village is undergoing something of a renaissance, with an ambitious land reclamation project consisting of a human-made island called Eve complete with facilities and jetty, to cope with increasing passenger and cargo traffic from Mahé. Tourists arrive at the jetty at the south end of the bay to be collected by a rash of taxis and tour operators that wakes the village from its sleepy existence. It's a good place to ease yourself into the rhythm of slow tropical life, stopping to chat to fishermen and locals in the small daily market. A narrow beach is backed by trees that provide shade, there are several banks, a few stores and Praslin's only hospital.

Southeast Praslin. Irregular buses travel the short distance between Côte d'Or beach, Vallée de Mai, Petite Anse and Baie Sainte Anne.

Côte d'Or or Anse Volbert

Praslin's main tourist beach, also known as Anse Volbert, is a 2km (1¼-mile) carpet of white sand bordered by clear shallow waters, making it ideal for children. Most activity centres on Anse Volbert, a laid-back village with a proliferation of hotels, guesthouses, shops, restaurants and casino cleverly concealed behind trees and swathed in tropical foliage. During the southeast monsoon, when seaweed covers the southern shores, this beach is especially popular with day-trippers from Grande Anse. Boat operators offer snorkelling

trips to the nearby islands of Chauve Souris and St Pierre, and days out to Curieuse, Cousin and Aride. There are a couple of places to hire a bike.
On Praslin's north coast, midway between Anse Possession and Anse Matelot.

Grande Anse

Occupying a long white strip of beach, Grande Anse is a busy little resort compared with Baie Sainte Anne and Côte d'Or mainly because most tour operators are based here. Only a few minutes' drive from the airport, this pretty resort has plenty of accommodation, from hotels to small guesthouses, and one or two cafés to give it a distinct village atmosphere. As in other parts of Praslin, nightlife is a low-key affair, apart from Friday and Saturday when islanders of all ages head for the **Briz Café** (*Tel: 233 454*) for takeaways before partying at the Oxygen Nightclub at Baie Sainte Anne.

Bus connections from Grande Anse to Vallée de Mai in the centre of the island or along the coast southwards take in views of the beaches of Anse Citron, Anse Bateau, Anse St Sauveur, Anse Takamaka, Anse Cimetière, Anse Bois de Rose and Anse Consolation. These are not ideal for swimming, but the golden sands and smooth brown boulders are picturesque and do merit a stop. The Indian Ocean Lodge (*see pp153–4*) at Grande Anse and the Coco de Mer Hotel at Anse Bois de Rose provide a free shuttle service for guests to Côte d'Or, a popular option during May to September when large expanses of seaweed cover the southern shores.
On the south coast, 3km (1³/₄ miles) east of the airport at Amitié.

Praslin and satellite islands

Chauve Souris Island from Côte d'Or

Praslin's satellite islands
Aride Special Nature Reserve

This 68ha (16-acre) island is the finest nature reserve of all the granitic islands of the Seychelles, where an abundance of breeding seabirds, rare endemic birds and unique plant life thrives in the most natural conditions. This most northerly of the granitic islands was bought by chocolate baron Christopher Cadbury in 1973 for the Royal Society for Nature Conservation and is so carefully managed that it is a conservationist's dream come true.

Landing takes place at La Cour beach in the south during safe weather conditions and needs a certain degree of sure-footedness. There is no jetty so you have to disembark from the main boat and into one of the island's 'clean'

A pair of local fairy terns grooming

dinghies to come ashore. You should wrap up valuables in plastic, wear shorts or swimwear, and carry a sensible pair of trainers as the paths on the island are steep, uneven and slippery after rains. Take water and something to eat because there are no refreshment facilities.

The island is leased and managed by the **Island Conservation Society**. The warden or one of his staff directs you to a Visitors' Shelter for the start of a guided nature trail that cuts through a former coconut plantation and settlement towards the coast. Look out for the rare Seychelles warbler, removed from the list of endangered birds following the transfer of 29 birds from Cousin in 1989. To the west, the path becomes very steep but here you will find the burrows of wedge-tailed shearwaters.

The guide will point out the Aride cucumber, which only flowers at night, and the Wright's gardenia, the only place in the world where it grows. Former Beatle, George Harrison, planted a Wright's gardenia in Mahé's Botanical Gardens in 2000 but it died soon after his death, and attempts to grow it on Mahé have never been successful. The flower is white and dotted with tiny pink streaks.

Aride has the world's largest concentration of lizards, and is alive with birdsong year-round. From March to November, there are lesser noddies and sooty terns; April to August sees the appearance of Roseate terns; and at

Cousin and Cousine Islands

other times of the year three species unique to the Seychelles – the sunbird, blue pigeon and the magpie robin can be seen along with giant primitive frigate birds and red-tailed tropicbirds.

Back at La Cour beach, you can go swimming or snorkelling, or enjoy a simple barbecue lunch if you have come with a tour operator. The reef is a treasure house for hundreds of fish, but always be aware of strong currents. *It takes 45 minutes by boat from Côte d'Or. Several tour operators and some hotels organise this excursion. The island is managed by the Island Conservation Society. Tel: 321 600. www.arideisland.net. Open: Sun & Wed. Trips during May to September depend on weather conditions.*

Cousin Island Nature Reserve

Cousin Island is a designated nature reserve, covers an area of 28ha (69 acres) and is one of the most popular excursions from Praslin. The voyage takes about 30 minutes from Baie Sainte Anne or a little longer from Côte d'Or. The boat anchors close to shore and you are transferred into a small boat. Landing involves getting your feet wet, so it's wise to wear shorts or swimwear and to pack cameras and other valuables in a plastic bag.

On Cousin, guides meet you for an informative 30-minute tour. Cousin is managed by Nature Seychelles and is a real treasure trove for birdwatchers and wildlife enthusiasts. Here you'll spot some of the Seychelles' rarest birds,

The fairy tern is a year-round fixture on Cousin

among them the Seychelles warbler, only recently rescued from the brink of extinction. Other birds to look out for are the magpie robin, the Seychelles fody and the Madagascar turtle dove. During the southeast monsoon, the lesser noddy swoops on the island and year-round the sky is dotted with graceful fairy terns.

Cousin used to be a coconut plantation before the Royal Society for Nature Conservation bought it as a nature reserve. All that remains are cotton, pawpaw and castor oil plants, and the only footprints you're likely to find on the sand are those of geckos, millipedes, a few giant Aldabra tortoises and two species of skink. During October to March, hawksbill turtles come to lay their eggs on the beach.

Masons Travel Praslin offers an exclusive full-day catamaran trip from Baie Sainte Anne. The excursion includes lunch, a visit to Curieuse, snorkelling on the islet of St Pierre and landing fees. Tel: 288 777.

Cousine Island
This tiny, privately owned islet to the south of Cousin attracts well-heeled honeymooners seeking total seclusion. Past guests include former Beatle, Sir Paul McCartney. Cousine can only cater for ten people at a time who stay in one of four old colonial-style beach-fronted villas. Distractions include birdwatching on the private reserve, where five endemic birds have made their home, or donning snorkel and mask to explore the colourful marine life.

Tel: 321 107. www.cousineisland.com.
By private transfer from Mahé airport
or Praslin.

Curieuse

Curieuse sits in a designated marine
park and is separated by a 1.5km
(1-mile) channel from Praslin's
northernmost point. The French called
the island Île Rouge because of the
exposed red earth still evident today,
but the name was changed to Curieuse
after a French ship, *La Curieuse*, visited
these waters in 1768. The island was a
former leper colony, and you can still
see the ruins at Anse Saint Jose on the
south coast and a renovated plantation
house used by the doctor from Praslin
who treated sufferers until 1965. It is
now an information centre.

A boardwalk from the information
centre leads through a mangrove
swamp, passing an abandoned pond,
to Laraie Baie where turtles, a much
prized delicacy, were once kept for
export. Nowadays, Curieuse is given
over to mature roaming giant
tortoises, descendants of the original
species on Aldabra. A Tortoise
Conservation Project set up to
preserve these prehistoric wonders
is at nearby Grande Anse where
their offspring are raised in safe
enclosures before being released into
the wild.

Masons Travel Praslin offers full-day
trips including Curieuse, lunch on
Cousin Island and snorkelling in the
marine park off the islet of St Pierre.
Tel: 288 777.

Praslin and satellite islands

Granite boulders on Curieuse

La Digue and satellite islands

Tiny La Digue is arguably the prettiest of all the Inner Islands, and film-makers and fashion photographers have used it as a perfect tropical island backdrop. For visitors, La Digue is an experience in going back in time and meeting a people renowned for their genuine friendliness.

La Digue

With just a few pickup trucks or *camions*, half a dozen ox-carts, four taxis and hundreds of bikes as the only means of transport for a population of 2,000, this is an island where walking is the best way to meet the people. Most are fisherfolk, farmers or employed in tourism, and to observe them cheerfully going about their daily business is precisely what sets La Digue apart from the other islands.

Laid-back locals in La Digue

La Digue is just 10sq km (3³/₄sq miles), or roughly four times the size of the City of London. Most people live at La Passe on the west coast, where daily ferries for Praslin come and go. There is a tourist office and there are dozens of guesthouses, all within walking distance of the jetty, and several small hotels.

Hugging the shore northwards from La Passe is a good coast road through jungly vegetation, passing the calm waters of the incongruously named Anse Severe. The road veers south to a collection of rocky bays, or *anses*, battered by rough seas during the southeast monsoon from May to September, and stops at Anse Banane where footpaths lead to more isolated coves.

Grande Anse, La Digue's biggest beach, is wild, rugged and dangerous, and notices in several languages attest to the powerful currents that have claimed lives. By contrast, Anse Source d'Argent, a short walk from La Passe, is the jewel in La Digue's crown.

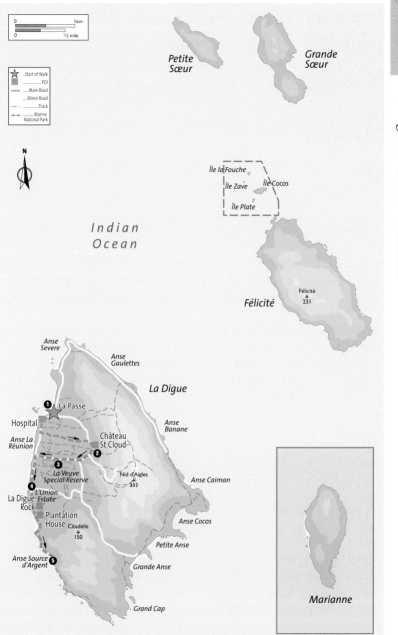

0   1km
0   1/2 mile

..Start of Walk
..................POI
.......Main Road
.....Minor Road
.........Track
.........Marine
National Park

N

Petite
Sœur

Grande
Sœur

Île la Fouche
Île Zave   Île Cocos
Île Plate

Indian
Ocean

Félicité
▲
231

Félicité

Anse
Severe

Anse
Gaulettes

La Digue

❶ La Passe

Hospital

Anse
Banane

Anse La
Réunion

Château
St Cloud

❷

❸
La Veuve
Special Reserve

Nid d'Aigles
▲
333

Anse Caiman

❹
L'Union Estate
La Digue
Rock

Plantation
House   Citadelle
▲
150

Anse Cocos

Petite Anse

Anse Source
d'Argent ❺

Grande Anse

Grand Cap

Marianne

Walk: La Digue

This 3km (2-mile) walk takes in the main sights and starts from La Passe.

Allow 1 hour on foot, or less if you go by bike.

See map on p75.

1 La Passe

La Digue's first settlers arrived at La Passe as exiles from Bourbon (the French island of Réunion) in 1798, following an uprising over taxation and rumours that it was to be handed over to the British. Today, La Passe is a lively village with a few restaurants and bars, a hospital, bike rental shops and a line of brightly painted ox-carts driven by happy-go-lucky Rastafarian youths.

Continue south, passing the hospital on your right, and take the first turning on your left. At 200m (220yds) is the Château St Cloud.

2 Château St Cloud

This grand colonial-style château, built in the early 19th century, sits at the top of a hill surrounded by houses and gardens bursting with breadfruit, mango and papaya trees. Named after the French town south of Paris, the château formed part of a vanilla estate and is owned by one of the island's oldest families. It is now a smart hotel, and the interior has been faithfully restored to its former glory.

Turn left outside the château and take the next main turning on the right to reach La Veuve Special Reserve.

3 La Veuve Special Reserve

It takes less than ten minutes to walk through the reserve noted for its large *takamaka* and Indian almond trees, both favourite nesting places for the paradise flycatcher. Locally known as *la veuve* (widow), the flycatcher has long black tail feathers not unlike a widow's veil. You may also see freshwater terrapins, the Seychelles moorhen and the cave swiftlet feeding on insects in a swampy area called La Soupape.

La Veuve Information Office. Tel: 234 353. Open: 8am–4pm. Free admission.
Turn left as you come out of the reserve and left again. Walk for 200m (220yds) to the entrance of L'Union Estate. Otherwise keep to the beach, which runs parallel with the estate.

4 L'Union Estate

This working estate produces vanilla, copra from the flesh of the coconut, and oil for cooking, perfumery and suntan products. Giant tortoises patrol an enclosure backed by La Digue Rock, a soaring granite boulder listed as a national monument. Like others in the Seychelles, it was formed by the slow cooling of magma and is part of the peaks left behind when the earth cooled 750 million years ago. The focal point is the thatched Plantation House (*see p79*), said to be the Seychelles' oldest, fronted by lawns leading directly to the beach.

L'Union Estate. Tel: 234 240.
Open: 7am–5pm. Admission charge.
Turn left at the beach for Anse Source d'Argent.

5 Anse Source d'Argent

Let your imagination run wild as you marvel at dozens of weird rock formations sculpted by the forces of nature, which frame a pathway to La Digue's most envied beach. Anse Source d'Argent, studded with granite boulders, is perfect for sunbathing. Even on the dullest of days it is so romantic that many couples choose this location to get married at sunset.
Retrace your steps to La Passe.

Walk: La Digue

Looming rocks at Anse Source d'Argent

Plantation houses

During the colonial period, the economy of the Seychelles relied entirely on the production of coconuts, vanilla and cinnamon. Planters lived in grand plantation houses with their families, but the ravages of tropical weather made maintenance costly and labour-intensive, and today only a few of these buildings survive.

A common feature of the Seychellois plantation house was the flight of steps on all four sides leading to a spacious veranda, which gave access to various rooms. The house was raised on blocks of coral or wood so that air could circulate freely, and the space beneath doubled as a storage area. The ground floor was made of timber boarding laid on floor joists, and the roof, woven from *latanier* leaves and giving it a thatched appearance, was supported by ridge poles and rafters made from the local hardwood, *takamaka*. Some of the grander houses had roofs made from *bardeaux*, or shingles, an age-old technique that involved cutting slices of hardwood into 1.25cm (½in) thick rectangles measuring 23cm × 10cm (9in × 4in). These roofs would last for years.

The *salon*, or sitting room, was the main living area, and the number of bedrooms with adjoining dressing rooms depended on the size of the

Typical Seychellois plantation house, Domaine de Val des Près

des Près, built a decade later, is also a museum with polished timber floors and high ceilings, and walls adorned with family portraits.

On La Digue, two out of the three plantation houses have been turned into hotels. The Yellow House, dating back to 1900, part of La Digue Island Lodge accommodation, has been converted into a collection of small rooms with spiral staircases leading down to spacious bathrooms. The Château St Cloud, a smart hotel, has been faithfully restored to its original beauty, complete with interior décor reflecting the grandeur of the colonial period. And finally there is the Plantation House, a listed national monument, on the copra and coconut plantation of L'Union Estate. It is said to be the oldest in the Seychelles and featured on the set of *Goodbye Emmanuel* in the early 1970s.

One of the most attractive plantation houses is on Silhouette Island, home to the Dauban family in the mid-18th century. The family owned the island and ran an 809ha (2,000-acre) coconut plantation employing 250 workers. In 2006, following thorough refurbishment, the house reopened as a restaurant for guests staying at the island's Labriz Hotel. Many of the original features are still in place, including a roof made from *bardeaux*.

Plantation house at La Digue

family. Bathrooms and toilets were placed away from the main building. The kitchen was always at the back of the house, usually as a separate annexe in case a fire broke out as food was cooked on open fires.

The servants' quarters were entirely separate from the main house. Maids and kitchen staff lived in simple timber huts with a thatched roof and were always on call to tend to the needs of the master and family.

Many plantation houses are privately owned, but there are some that can be visited. In Mahé there is L'Enfoncement in Jardin du Roi at Anse aux Pins. Built in 1860, it is now a museum containing antique furnishings and memorabilia reminiscent of bygone days. The Plantation House at Domaine de Val

La Digue's satellite islands

Boats from the jetty at La Passe make day trips to the satellite islands to the northeast of La Digue. Rising like flooded mountain peaks of a lost continent with underwater valleys and caves, these islands provide a natural habitat for myriad marine species. You may spot inquisitive shoals of parrotfish, sweetlips and groupers and even whale sharks during November. All the islands, apart from Félicité, can also be visited from Praslin.

Félicité

Félicité Island is 3km (1³/₄ miles) northeast of La Digue. This private island has lush forests and superb beaches, and is undergoing major

La Penice beach, Félicité Island

tourism redevelopment with 66 designer hilltop residences targeted at foreign buyers and investors. Called **Zil Pasyon**, the Creole term for Isle of Passion, resort visitors will have access to a watersports centre, tennis courts, fine dining, infinity swimming pools and the world's first Rock Wine Cave – a wine cellar carved into a natural rock façade. To complete the luxury experience there will be a Per Aquum spa for essential pampering and a private helicopter pad. Expected to open in July 2011.
www.zilpasyon.com

Grande Sœur and Petite Sœur

The Morel family of Praslin owns the two islets of Grande and Petite Sœur, which lie 2km (1¹/₄ miles) to the north of Félicité Island. Grande Sœur has two sparkling coral-fringed beaches and is the Morel family home, while Petite Sœur, a third of the size of its big sister, is uninhabited and landing is difficult because it has no beach.
From La Digue: Your hotel or guesthouse can organise day trips, including snorkelling and barbecue, during the week to Grande Sœur.
From Praslin: The Morel family also owns Château de Feuilles Hotel (see p154), and at weekends the island is reserved for the exclusive use of guests. The hotel offers a complimentary excursion with a barbecue, leaving by boat from Baie Sainte Anne. Hotels in Praslin can arrange mid-week visits.

Île Cocos and the La Digue Island Lodge excursion boat

Île Cocos, Île la Fouche, Île Plate and Île Zave

Just 0.5km (¼ mile) off Félicité's northern shores is the minuscule Île Cocos, encircled by a coral reef. From the sea, verdant palms seem to pop out of the turquoise waters which are studded with smooth boulders, and the area is excellent for snorkelling. During the 1980s, the waters were almost depleted of coral by tourists and visits were banned. Thankfully, mother nature has come to the rescue and the corals are recovering. Île de la Fouche, Île Zave and Île Plate nearby are no more than protrusions of granite and the habitat of seabirds, including the wedge-tailed shearwater, the bridled tern and the lesser noddy.

Masons Travel on La Digue, your hotel or guesthouse can arrange a trip to these islands.

Marianne

Like Petite Sœur, this island is uninhabited. It is 5km (3 miles) east of Félicité's southern coast, and a mantle of coconut palms covers this dot of a granite island. Much of the native forest has disappeared along with a host of endemic birds, but the north end is showing signs of regeneration. With only two beaches, landing by small boats can only take place in the west, which is protected by a coral reef. *Masons Travel on La Digue, your hotel or guesthouse can arrange a trip to Marianne.*

Honeymoon havens

The Seychelles ooze romance, with picture-postcard beaches, swaying palm trees, year-round ocean breezes and a sun-blessed climate. However, this destination is not just for honeymoons – the islands are full of romantic retreats and romantics holding hands along deserted beaches or doing the simple things in life like taking time out to be with their partners.

Cerf Island Resort

At Cerf Island Lodge in Sainte Anne Marine Park, honeymooners receive a personal welcome and get to stay in spacious lodges with views of Mahé's twinkling lights. The romantic

Desroches Island Resort

restaurant, hilltop spa and circular pool complement lazy days spent on the beach and trips to neighbouring islands.
Sainte Anne National Marine Park, c/o PO Box 1071, Victoria. Tel: 294 500. Fax: 294 511. Email: info@cerf-resort.com. www.cerf-resort.com

Denis Island Resort

Denis, only a 30-minute flight from Mahé, is one of those havens noted for the back-to-nature experience with oodles of luxury. You stay in an air-conditioned Creole-style chalet complete with four-poster bed and a private veranda overlooking your own garden and beach. The absence of TV, radio and cars conspires to lull you into a silent cocooned world broken only by the sound of birdsong, and where even work can't buzz you on your Blackberry.
Denis Island, c/o PO Box 404, Victoria. Tel: 295 999. Fax: 321 010. Email: info@denisisland.com. www.denisisland.com

Desroches Island Resort

For a far-flung honeymoon destination, Desroches Island in the Amirantes group takes some beating.

A romantic four-poster at the Denis Island Resort

Twenty-four villas with four-poster beds, outdoor bathrooms and private sea-facing terraces assure total privacy. The island, a former coconut plantation, has some lovely trails to explore on foot or bicycle, and there's excellent diving. At night, you dine beneath the stars beside the stunning pool or moonlit beach.
c/o PO Box 378, Victoria, Mahé. Tel: 229 003. Fax: 229 002. Email: desroches.res@seychelles.net. www.desroches-island.com

Hilton Seychelles Northolme Resort and Spa
If you're after the buzz of nightlife rather than the buzz of the birds and bees, the Hilton on Mahé's west coast attracts trendy young couples to a contemporary shot of fun and frolics from decked terraces. Small sandy coves and an islet for private dining, complete with views of Silhouette and North islands, provide an intimate touch.
Glacis, Mahé. Tel: 299 000. Fax: 299 001. www.hiltonworldresorts.com

Lemuria Resort
The Lemuria Resort on Praslin's northwest coast is another romantic retreat offering a gorgeous selection of suites. If you want to push the boat out, go for an enormous private villa with a sunken dining area surrounded by water features, private massage pavilion and decked terraces, and let the villa master prepare your meals, organise excursions or book you into the spa for pre- or post-nuptial pampering. You could try golf on the challenging 18-hole course in the resort or take dreamy walks to the deserted beaches of Anse Georgette and Anse Kerlan.
Anse Kerlan. Tel: 281 281. Fax: 281 001. Email: resa@lemuriaresort.com. www.lemuriaresort.com

Maia Resort
The Maia Resort claims 6-star luxury with a spa to die for. Set in a superb clifftop location, these swish and seriously spacious villas come with a plunge pool, jacuzzi and private butler.
Anse Louise, Mahé. Tel: 390 000. Fax: 390 010. www.maia.com.sc

Denis Island

A 30-minute flight from Mahé brings you to crescent-shaped Denis, one of only two coralline islands (the other is Bird) within the Inner Islands group.

For walk, see p86.

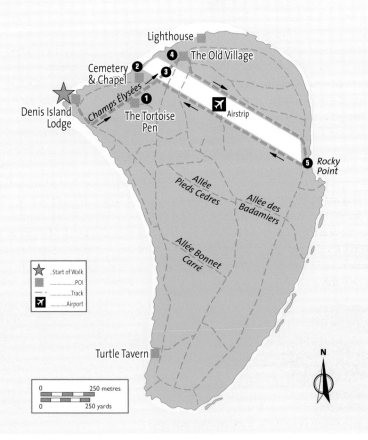

Lighthouse

The Old Village

Cemetery & Chapel ❷

❹

❸

Denis Island Lodge

Champs Élysées

❶

The Tortoise Pen

Airstrip

❺ Rocky Point

Allée Pieds Cedres

Allée des Badamiers

Allée Bonnet Carré

..Start of Walk
..................POI
...............Track
..........Airport

Turtle Tavern

0   250 metres
0   250 yards

N

Denis was a former coconut plantation and is now developed for ecotourism, attracting honeymooners, nature lovers and birdwatchers. The island is 1.3km (³/₄ mile) long and 1.75km (1 mile) at its widest point and perfectly walkable. There is only one place to stay – the enchanting Denis Island Resort (*see p82*).

The plane bumps along a palm-bordered grassy runway, seemingly in the middle of a great ocean. You are met by staff from the hotel and driven in an electric buggy to your chalet where the dream of luxury desert-island living unfolds.

This privately owned island is off-limits to day-trippers. Although you can spend one night here, you're encouraged to stay for three to simply unwind and relax on your own beach, listening to birdsong, gazing at the antics of brilliant green geckos darting amid tropical foliage and tiny crabs scurrying across white sands. Being on the edge of the Seychelles fishing bank where the ocean floor drops to 2,000m (6,500ft), it's also popular with big game fishermen, and the chances of hooking your own fish are high. Just tag it and

BIRD ISLAND

Bird Island is a haven for birds. Lying 96km (60 miles) north of Mahé, like its closest neighbour, Denis, 46.5km (29 miles) to the east, it too has been developed for ecotourism. From May to October, sooty terns and at least 20 other species appear, hawksbill and green turtles come ashore to lay their eggs, the lagoon fringed by a coral reef is a kaleidoscope of marine life, and the island is home to one of the world's largest tortoises, the tame male Esmeralda. Guests staying at the island's only accommodation, the Bird Island Lodge, can get involved with turtle tagging programmes and enjoy fresh food produced on the island.

have it cooked to order by the resident chef. Other must-do's include windsurfing, canoeing and snorkelling, boat trips around the island, sunset cruises and magical diving.

As a guest, you are expected to be part of the barefoot luxury experience and wander at will. There are no keys to your room, mobile phones don't work, there is no TV, you eat organic food prepared from produce grown on the island farm and fish caught daily from the lagoon, and you're certainly not expected to wear your best bib and tucker for dinner.

The grass runway is clearly visible as you approach Denis Island

Walk: Denis

This 3km (1¾-mile) walk takes 1 hour along flat paths bounded by luxuriant vegetation.

Start from the Lodge reception area and follow the path marked 'Champs Élysées'.

See map on p84.

1 The Tortoise Pen

After about 100m (110yds), on the right is a healthy colony of Aldabra giant tortoises. Look for Toby, weighing in at 197kg (434lb), and girlfriend Clara who goes on regular walkabouts. She's partial to villa no 28 where she spends the day cooling herself beneath the air-conditioning equipment.

Denis Island chapel

After about 150m (165yds), on your left along Champs Élysées is a cemetery and small chapel.

2 Cemetery and chapel

Nobody knows who lies in the nameless 18th-century graves as no official burial records exist, although stories abound of treasure. In 1978, Denis' previous owner, Pierre Burkhardt, a French industrialist, built the small chapel next door for the estate workers. Today, foreign couples get married here amid joyful birdsong, and it's also a rare day out for resident estate staff who turn up to be blessed by the visiting priest from Mahé.

Turn left, passing staff quarters on your right, to reach the grassy runway.

3 The airstrip

The airstrip slices the island in two. It is 900m (990yds) long and runs from southeast to northwest. The turnaround time for aircraft is about 15 minutes, and happy-go-lucky firemen appear in protective clothing

Soaking timber is a tested way of disinfecting it

for routine checks. In 2000, the island was infested with rats, posing a serious health hazard and threat to birdlife, but they have now been eliminated. To keep it that way, heavy supplies are brought ashore by landing craft to the north of a runway, a large tarpaulin is spread on the beach and the area is rigorously checked to ensure no rats have got a free ride. All rubbish on the island is collected and transported to Mahé for disposal.

Cross the runway, watching out for aircraft. The Old Village is immediately on the other side.

4 The Old Village

Denis used to be a copra plantation, and the former buildings are now offices and outhouses where the 80 resident staff live and work. The present owners aim to restore the ecosystem close to its original form by proper conservation management. They have succeeded in that they have become self-sufficient, providing the Lodge with essential needs – and more. Carpenters make furniture from the *takamaka* and casuarina trees that grow here; organic produce is grown using an irrigation system; a hydroponic greenhouse is in place; a piggery, henhouse and cows provide food; and there is even an eco-friendly desalination and diesel power plant. To the north is a lighthouse erected in 1905.

Walk the length of the runway, and turn right for Rocky Point and woodlands.

5 Rocky Point and woodlands

Here, piles of seaweed brought in from the southeast monsoon are collected and dried for fertiliser. Logs of the casuarina trees are left in sea water at Rocky Point for several months. This disinfecting process ensures that the future timber will be disease- and termite-free. The woodland is full of Indian almond trees that are used for construction and provide a good source of food for birds.

Retrace your steps to the Lodge.

Silhouette Island

Silhouette is the third-largest island of the Seychelles, and with fewer than 200 residents is the least populated. It has the second-highest mountain, Mont Dauban, at 751m (2,464ft). Its thickly wooded slopes are the habitat of over 2,000 species of flora and fauna; scientists regard it as one of the most important biodiversity hotspots of the Indian Ocean. In 2010 it was declared a national park.

In 1860, Silhouette became the property of wealthy French settler Auguste Dauban, who built stone paths, still evident today, that take in some lovely nature walks. Successive generations of his family turned the island into a coconut plantation, later growing fruit trees and spices until it was sold in 1970 to a French consortium and developed for tourism.

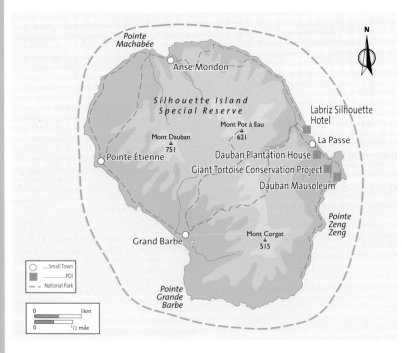

Giant Tortoise Conservation Project

This project is run by Nature Protection Trust Seychelles, which aims to preserve the natural habitat of Silhouette and to restore degraded areas to their natural state. The Trust is having huge success in saving the Seychelles saddle back and the Seychelles domed giant, two species of giant tortoise thought to have been extinct for 150 years. In 1997, six of each species were brought to Silhouette from Aldabra Island, and they bred happily in enclosures, producing youngsters that have now been released into the wild. Visitors are welcome to visit the centre where there are shell collections, specimens of insects and plants, and information on similar programmes for the Seychelles terrapin and hawksbill turtle.

100m (110yds) south from the Plantation House. Open: 10am–4pm.

La Passe

Little remains of the Dauban legacy apart from the family mausoleum built on the architectural lines of the Madeleine in Paris. New housing developments and social amenities in the village meet 21st-century chic in the luxurious chalets of Labriz Silhouette Hotel that overlook a pristine white beach. Even La Grande Case, the Dauban family plantation house, was transformed into a romantic restaurant without losing any of its original beauty. Guests dine

NORTH ISLAND

North Island, 7km (4¹/₂ miles) north of Silhouette, is a haven for affluent conservation-conscious visitors who land by helicopter. The only place to stay is the private North Island Lodge, voted in 2006 by *Conde Nast* readers as the 'best hotel in the world'. With just 11 villas, the island is a sanctuary where natural habitats are being restored for the reintroduction of critically endangered species, such as the blue pigeon and Seychelles white eye. There are 22 dive sites to explore too.

North Island Lodge. Tel: 293 100.
www.north-island.com. Bookings essential.
Flights can be arranged through Air Seychelles helicopter services (Tel: 385 863).

on the veranda or indoors on cooler evenings.

La Passe is on the east coast. Big Blue Divers at Beau Vallon, Mahé, organise day dive trips around Silhouette Island. (Tel: 261 106). Air Seychelles helicopter flights also make the 15-minute trip. Tel: 385 863.

Giant tortoises saved by the conservation project

Silhouette Island

Giant tortoises

The Aldabra giant tortoise (*Geochelone gigantean*) is one of the biggest in the world and similar in size to those found in the Galápagos. The carapace measures approximately 120cm (47in) and it has an average weight of 250kg (551lb). The neck can expand to 1m (3ft) and reaches out like a crane to grab food in high places. In the remote and inhospitable islands of Aldabra, where it really is a matter of the survival of the fittest, this chelonian, unlike its vegetarian cousins, chomps away at anything and even dabbles in cannibalism.

Giant tortoises once roamed many of the western Indian Ocean islands,

Caroline the tortoise on Desroches Island

but their population dwindled as seamen on long voyages of discovery realised that they had stumbled upon a source of fresh meat. In 1609, John Jourdain, an agent of the East India Company aboard the *Ascension*, drifted to the Seychelles noting that 'the tortelles were good meat as good as fresh meat', and over the next two centuries thousands were carried off. Most were sold by entrepreneurs in Mauritius and the Seychelles and consigned to on-board cooking pots, while others were lucky enough to be presented as gifts to colonial governors in Mauritius and as far away as Saint Helena in the south Atlantic.

The first serious conservation efforts began in 1874 when Charles Darwin petitioned the governor of Mauritius for the protection of the species. Nevertheless, tortoise farms continued to offer the captured giants for sale. In the early 1960s, the tortoises' fate was almost sealed when the Americans planned to build an air base on Aldabra, but, following international protest, the project was shelved and today Aldabra is home to 150,000 tortoises, the world's largest population.

Giant tortoise pen at Victoria Botanical Gardens

Aldabra tortoises are still kept as pets and given names by the Seychellois. When a female child is born, the parents present her with a baby tortoise. Thankfully, the tradition of eating the family pet when the girl got married has now ceased. In other parts of the world, tortoises are highly valued as pets and can fetch prices of up to $US20,000, depending on size and weight.

Giant tortoises are so fascinating that many have become famous. Gordon, a gift to a British governor in the Seychelles in 1881, was believed to have reached his 200th birthday when he was still upsetting games of croquet on the lawns of Government House. In 1956 on Cousin Island, George, a usually tame type, disgraced himself when he tried to nip the hand of the exiled Archbishop Makarios. Meanwhile, Esmeralda on Bird Island, who continues to amuse visitors, once made it into the Guinness Book of Records as the world's heaviest tortoise at 304kg (670lb).

Tortoises tend to outlive humans and many myths surround their longevity, although carbon-dating techniques may one day determine their true age. One of the oldest in recent times was Adwaitya who, according to records, was 255 years old when he died in 2006 in Kolkata (Calcutta) Zoo. Adwaitya, which means 'the only one', was brought from the Seychelles as a gift for Robert Clive of India and certainly lived up to his name as the zoo's unique attraction.

Frégate Island

Lying 55km (34 miles) east of Mahé and covering 3sq km (1sq mile), Frégate, like other islands in the Seychelles, saw its time out as a coconut plantation. In 1998, it was developed as a 'one island one resort' destination, and counts film stars and footballers among its celebrity guest list.

Guests arrive by helicopter from Mahé, landing at the airstrip in the northeast. With seven sparkling beaches, electric cars to get around, a private marina and 16 villas to entice the well-heeled, this island is synonymous with a secluded, luxurious lifestyle. Much of the food is organically grown on the island and turned into delicious dishes at the restored Plantation House restaurant.

The resident conservationist offers nature walks for those willing to leave

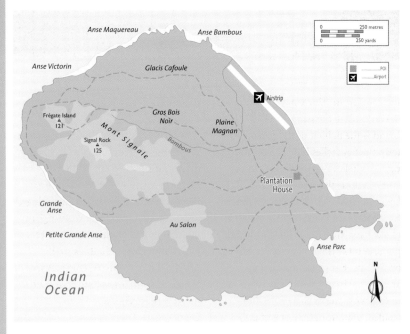

Aerial view of Frégate Island

the comfort of their villas, or you may like to explore the paths yourself. The island is the habitat of the Seychelles fody, the Seychelles blue pigeon and the rare Seychelles magpie robin. Other fauna include the giant tenebrionid beetle, a large flightless creature looking for all the world as though a child has glued it together from different insect parts, and Gardiner's gecko, found only on Frégate. On your meanderings around the island, you'll also come face to face with one or two of the 400 resident giant tortoises, one of only three wild roaming populations left in the Seychelles.

You can spend lazy days windsurfing, sailing, snorkelling and diving. The best diving for sightings of moray eels, octopus, scorpion fish and lots of reef fish is in the marine-rich waters fringed by a protective coral reef at Anse Parc in the southeast. Other superb beaches in the north for sunbathing and relaxing include Anse Victorin, Anse Maquereau and Anse Bambous, and, in the west, Grande and Petite Grande Anse.

Island celebrities past and present

In 1502, celebrity sailor and Portuguese explorer Vasco da Gama scored top marks for sighting a remote collection of islands southwest of Mahé, which he called the Amirantes. He could hardly have known that over five centuries later the Seychelles would become a favourite haunt for the rich, the famous and the infamous.

There was little chance of escape for the rulers, royalty and a Greek Orthodox priest who were banished here by the Brits. Yet hard times in paradise passed smoothly for the Sultan of Perak who dropped by in 1875 after being implicated in the murder of a British citizen. It was a tolerable experience too for Prempeh, King of the Ashanti, who arrived in style in 1900 with wives and kids and stayed for 24 years. In 1956, the 'A' list encompassed Archbishop Makarios of Cyprus, whose must-do's included climbing the mountains of Mahé in voluminous black robes, and the Pahlavi family, ex-rulers of Iran before the revolution, who fled their

The Banyan Tree Resort, on land once owned by George Harrison and Peter Sellers

country to live on D'Arros Island in the Amirantes.

In the 1970s, former Beatle George Harrison and actor Peter Sellers fell in love with the Seychelles and bought a chunk of land now occupied by the Banyan Tree Resort in Mahé. Nowadays, stars from Hollywood and Bollywood are content to flit in and out of paparazzi-free zones like Frégate or Cousine.

Félicité is very exclusive. It saw Pierce Brosnan come back to earth from his role as James Bond in the filming of *The World is Not Enough*, and rumour has it that Michael Douglas and Catherine Zeta Jones breezed by along with Brad Pitt and Jennifer Aniston. It's the sort of bolt hole where you could spend your holiday celebrity-spotting while brushing up your Microsoft skills with Bill Gates.

Although the film *Titanic* made it to Mahé's cinema, locals didn't recognise Leonardo DiCaprio shopping in town, apart from one love-sick Seychellois teenager who swooned at the sight of the star's sun-bleached hair. And in 2008 the Emir of Qatar, a regular visitor to Seychelles, deployed an armada of private yachts and a super-jet to get himself and his entourage to the Outer Islands for a spot of fishing.

Seychelles has its own brand of celebrities leading eclectic and

Anse Source d'Argent, location for *Castaway*

colourful lives. Brendon Grimshaw, former British newspaper editor, bought Moyenne Island in 1970 and still lives there, welcoming visitors washed ashore (*see pp55–6*). His book, *A Grain of Sand*, recounts how he came to be in the Seychelles and is essential reading for insights into what makes the Seychellois tick.

In 2010, Kantilal Jivan, aka 'Renaissance Man' by friends and fans suddenly passed away at the age of 87. A great writer, historian, guru, thinker, natural medicine practitioner and relentless pioneer of environmentalism and ecotourism, he will be sorely missed by regular visitors at his humble downtown drapery store in Victoria where he would read palms and recount stories of encounters with royalty and film stars.

Outer Islands: Alphonse and Amirantes groups

The Outer Islands consist of 72 low-lying sand cays and coral atolls. Southwest of Mahé is the Aldabra group with the island of Assomption and atolls of Aldabra, Astove and Cosmoledo, and the Farquhar group with the atolls of Providence and Farquhar. South of Mahé is the Southern Coral group of Platte and Coetivy. Closest to Mahé are the Alphonse and Amirantes groups.

Silhouette

Rémire

Inner Islands

Mahé

Amirantes Group

D'Arros

St Joseph

Desroches

Poivre Atoll

Marie Louise

Indian
Ocean

Platte

Desnœufs

Alphonse

Alphonse Group

Bijoutier

Saint François

N

0		100km
0		60 miles

Alphonse group

The Alphonse group of islands includes Alphonse, Bijoutier and Saint François. Alphonse is 400km (250 miles) southwest of Mahé and was named after Chevalier Alphonse de Pontevez, commander of the French vessel, *Le Lys*, who discovered the island in 1730. The flight from Mahé takes one hour, and from the air the island looks like a giant manta ray skimming the surface of a turquoise lagoon. The island used to be a coconut plantation before it was turned over to tourism, and you can still see the old ruins of the copra dryers and visit a cemetery containing the graves of people who worked on the island. One of the oldest graves is that of Henri Joseph who died in the 19th century and was believed to have been a freed African slave who came to work on the plantation.

Swimming in the lagoon is safe and rewarding as algae-covered rocks and seaweed provide ideal habitats for myriad fish to feed and breed, and there are wonderful excursions to the sandbanks of Saint François and Bijoutier islands. The only place to stay is Alphonse Island Resort, closed to traditional beach holidays until late 2011, but open to small groups of fly fishermen who can base themselves here for excursions to neighbouring Saint François.

Alphonse Island and lagoon

Outer Islands: Alphonse and Amirantes groups

Excursions to the Alphonse group of islands

Bijoutier

Just 5km (3 miles) south from Alphonse is tiny Bijoutier, which means 'tiny jewel'. Rising from turquoise waters and crowned with verdant foliage, it really does live up to its name. This island can be visited from Alphonse as a day trip with experienced crew, but it takes some getting to as you have to cross the treacherous currents of Canal la Mort, or 'death channel', to get there.

405km (252 miles) southwest of Mahé.

Saint François

Saint François is the most southerly of the Alphonse islands and was named after Saint Francis de Sales, a French Roman Catholic bishop. A dangerous reef studded with the remains of shipwrecks rings the island, but you can enter safely into its enormous lagoon with an experienced sailor through the pass known as La Passe Traversée. A mangrove swamp circling the shores is the habitat of grey herons and whimbrels, while crabs scurry across the sands. To the south of Saint François, beyond the reef, the wall drops dramatically, making it one of the deepest in the Indian Ocean. The lagoon and submerged sandbanks attract North American fly-fishing enthusiasts who make the 30-minute journey by boat from Alphonse. Currently there is no accommodation on Saint François but there are plans to build a luxurious fishing hideaway complete with tents on the beach.

410km (255 miles) southwest of Mahé.

Excursions to the Amirantes group of islands

The Amirantes group includes 25 islands strung over 95km (59 miles) from African Banks in the north to Desnœufs in the south. This group is the closest to Mahé and includes the privately owned islands of Rémire and D'Arros, the atolls

The Alphonse Island Resort

of Poivre and Saint Joseph, Marie Louise and Desroches. Many of these islands are owned by the government and are protected areas for bird and marine life, but they can be visited by private yacht provided you have permission. Only Desroches (*see pp102–3*) has tourist accommodation and can be reached by regular flights from Mahé.

D'Arros

D'Arros has one guesthouse occupying an oval-shaped platform reef and, with the 13 islets of neighbouring Saint Joseph Atoll making up less than 1sq km (²/₅sq mile) of land, is a closely guarded bolt hole for politicians, oil tycoons and the rich and famous.
255km (158 miles) southwest of Mahé.

Desnœufs

The most southerly of the Amirantes, Desnœufs is a protected breeding reserve for sooty terns which come in vast numbers to lay their eggs. The eggs are a delicacy in Mahé but collecting is government controlled to allow the birds to breed successfully.
325km (202 miles) southwest of Mahé.

Marie Louise

This 0.25sq km (¹/₁₀sq mile) island seems to crop up on most sailing itineraries of the Amirantes. However, although there is an airstrip to serve the few inhabitants, there is no regular transport or accommodation.
310km (193 miles) southwest of Mahé.

Bijoutier, the 'tiny jewel'

Poivre Atoll

This atoll includes three islands, Poivre, South Island and Florentin, all former coconut plantations and surrounded by waters that attract divers and serious deep-sea fishing enthusiasts. Only Poivre has a small settlement, and there are plans to turn it into a luxury island resort.
270km (168 miles) southwest of Mahé.

Rémire

Unless you're on a private yacht and get the necessary permission to land, few visitors make it ashore to Rémire. This beautiful islet, hemmed in by white beaches and brimming with woodland, is a tiny platform reef of less than 0.5sq km (¹/₅sq mile) and is the private home of former President Albert René.
245km (152 miles) west of Mahé.

Cruising around islands

Although Mahé, Praslin and La Digue have become exotic holiday destinations, there are many islands in the Seychelles yet to be discovered. The best way to see them is to charter a yacht, with or without crew, and visit the islands in comfort, without the pain and hardship experienced by early adventurers and explorers.

The Inner Islands are blessed with leisurely sailing conditions and are easily accessible by yacht or catamaran. The **Marine Charter**

Catch a 'cat' from Anse Major, Mahé

Association (*Tel: 322 126*) in Mahé, an umbrella organisation of yachting and charter companies based a few minutes from Victoria centre, offers day cruises and longer excursions to many islands providing safe havens and romantic hideaways. You can cruise to the islands of Sainte Anne Marine Park, off the east coast, Conception and Thérèse on the west coast, and North and Silhouette islands in the northwest. Praslin and La Digue and their satellite islands, and Bird and Denis are only a few hours away from Mahé, and all you need to do is relax and enjoy the views.

If you are based on Praslin and fancy some personalised cruising of the satellite islands, two catamarans, the *Charming Lady* and *Summer's Day*, operate from the **Hotel Coco de Mer** at Anse Bois de Rose (*Tel: 290 555. www.cocodemer.com*). The two-night cruises start from €1,600 per person, and you can swim with turtles and rays, laze on the deck or enjoy lunch in secluded bays. Each catamaran has six spacious double en-suite cabins, all meals and soft drinks are provided, and the multi-lingual skipper and crew make knowledgeable guides.

Denis Island is easily reached by boat from Mahé

Also on Praslin is **Dream Yacht Charters** (*Tel: 232 681. www.dreamyachtcharter.com*) where fully equipped modern catamarans and mono hulls are available for bareboat, crewed or day charter. They can take up to 16 people on Inner Island cruises or cruises to the Amirantes in the Outer Islands. Prices for a seven-night cruise start from €1,061 per person.

Cruising to the Outer Islands requires more time, expertise and a sense of adventure. The rewards are great when you reach the Amirantes and Alphonse groups, a chain of islands that includes Desroches and Alphonse, with tiny Bijoutier and Saint François, and the lesser-visited D'Arros, Desnœufs and Poivre where fishing, diving and snorkelling in these marine-rich waters put a whole new dimension on the meaning of sport.

The UNESCO World Heritage Site of Aldabra, the Seychelles' most precious asset, is accessible by private yacht, but you will need to get permission to land from the **Seychelles Islands Foundation** (*Tel: 321 735. www.sif.sc*), which manages the islands and complies with regulations. Alternatively, **Ocean Charters** (*Tel: 711 100, www.oceancharters.sc*) offer several cruises of a lifetime to the Amirantes and beyond aboard the *Lady Gabrielle*, a luxury 4-berth 42-foot catamaran, or can tailor-make a cruise to the Inner Islands. Expect to pay around €2,700 for overnight charters.

Some islands in marine national parks or nature reserves have restricted landing access. Others are privately owned or are managed by the para-statal Island Development Company and also attract access, landing and overnight fees. If you go on an organised cruise, these formalities are normally arranged, but otherwise you should check with the island before setting off to avoid any problems.

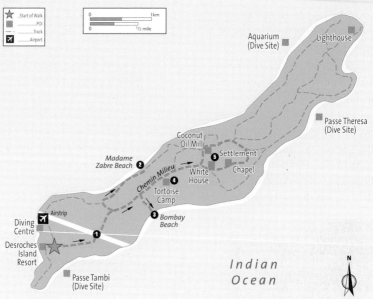

Desroches Island

Desroches is just 6km (3½ miles) long and barely 1km (⅔ mile) across and forms part of the Amirantes, a group of coral islands lying 230km (143 miles) southwest of Mahé. The island is a huge coconut plantation, and going there is like entering a time warp where workers still use traditional methods to collect coconuts, which are turned into copra for export to Mahé.

Normally, the direct flight from Mahé takes 45 minutes, or a little longer if the plane stops at Alphonse to pick up passengers. The flight alone is breathtaking, passing over a seascape dotted with beach-belted green islands fashioned in weird and wonderful shapes and surrounded by spectacular wide reefs and turquoise lagoons.

Desroches Island Resort, the only place to stay, is noted for fine dining under the stars and an imaginative chef who provides regular supplies to pampered castaways. The Resort has 46 comfortable suites and villas, each supplied with two bicycles and hidden beneath perfectly shaped coconut trees and a white sandy beach. The only way of getting around is by foot or bike along well-kept paths. Visitors arriving by plane are met by the manager and escorted into the colonial-style reception area fronting a swimming pool for a welcome drink.

For die-hard romantics, desert island fans and nature lovers Desroches is the ultimate escape. Apart from the beaches you can visit the Island Conservation Society office at Settlement where guests are encouraged to participate in turtle monitoring and other conservation projects. Children will love petting baby Aldabra tortoises in the adjacent enclosure while divers are treated to magnificent reef dives to see the habitats of hawksbill turtles and black tip reef sharks. *See p104 for tour.*

Excursions to the Outer Islands: dive and snorkelling sites

The Outer Islands of the Seychelles are all coralline or sand cays and offer impressive diving opportunities. Only Alphonse and Desroches in the Amirantes (*see p97 and opposite*) have accommodation and dive centres with excursions to sites rich in marine life, shipwrecks and some of the finest Gorgonian fan corals imaginable.

(*Cont. on p106*)

Honeymooners can have the place to themselves on Desroches

Outer Islands: Alphonse and Amirantes groups

Cycling tour: Settlement, Desroches

This route takes you to Settlement in the centre of the island and provides insights into plantation life. There's not much else beyond Settlement other than forests of casuarina trees and a lighthouse at the tip of the island.

This tour covers 6km (3½ miles). Allow 20 minutes if cycling or 1 hour and 30 minutes if you decide to walk.

See map on p102.

1 The airstrip

From the hotel reception building, follow the track, passing hotel staff quarters on your right and then cross the airstrip. Flights arrive and leave daily, sometimes twice, depending on the number of guests, so take care when crossing. There is a chain preventing access to the airstrip during flight arrivals, but at other times you can cycle the 1km (⅔-mile) length.

Cycling on Desroches Island

Cross the airstrip and continue to the coconut plantation along Chemin Milieu to Madame Zabre Beach.

2 Madame Zabre Beach

Chemin Milieu is the path that cuts through the middle of the island passing through a deeply wooded coconut plantation. Some 300m (330yds) along this path there is a sign on the left to Madame Zabre Beach. This beach has a shallow lagoon and is particularly good for snorkelling. Dabble your toes here or just take a rest, watching out for large land crabs burrowing into the sand. *Return to Chemin Milieu and continue for another 300m (330yds), looking out for a sign on your right to Bombay Beach.*

3 Bombay Beach

This side of the island can get very windy during the southeast monsoon from May to October, when seaweed collects on the beach. At other times, it is calm. Nearby are a few workers' houses and a sawmill, where

Houses on stilts at Settlement

coconut and casuarina trees are cut up for timber.

Retrace your route back to Chemin Milieu, passing through more coconut plantations; on your right is a tortoise camp.

4 Tortoise Camp

This large enclosure has a handful of giant land tortoises. They are looked after by the copra workers and are penned in to prevent them from straying across the airstrip. Two of them, George and Caroline, are tame enough to make regular appearances by the hotel beach where they loiter for goodies at breakfast time.

Continue for another 500m (550yds) to the main T-junction for Settlement.

5 Settlement

There's a worn, neglected village feel about Settlement, with its buildings scattered beneath coconut trees. Here, 15 contract workers from Mahé on six-monthly government contracts spend their time collecting coconuts, which are turned into copra. You can see the storehouse or drying shed containing sacks of coconuts and a working furnace just beside the sparkling white beach. The workers live in green-roofed A-frame houses raised on stilts; there is a recreational area, football and volleyball pitch and a public telephone box, but not much else for them to do. Other activities include growing produce for the hotel and raising pigs, which are exported to Mahé. In the middle of Settlement stands the former manager's plantation house, grandly known as the White House. Nearby are the offices of the Island Conservation Society.

Retrace your route back to Desroches Island Resort.

The snorkelling too is not to be missed. Dive centres offer two-hour excursions in the shallow lagoon or further afield. Die-hards can enjoy a half-day foray, returning in time for lunch. However, Alphonse Island is closed until late 2011 for complete refurbishment.

On Desroches, you can charter a private boat for a half or full day (*from the Boat House, next door to the diving centre*), sailing to waters frequented by tuna, bonito, kingfish and sailfish. It's not uncommon to return with a record catch, but you should check that the boat is not undergoing routine maintenance before you arrive on the island to avoid disappointment.

Alice in Wonderland
This site to the east of Alphonse teems with huge numbers of reef fish and sea creatures, including twin spotted snappers, sweetlips, Napoleon wrasse and green turtles. The corals are alive with tiny shimmering orange basse. In the deeper waters you are likely to see dogtooth tuna and eagle rays.

Astove
The remote site of Astove in the Aldabra group, accessible only by private yacht charter, reveals 3m (10ft) Gorgonian fans and massive barrel sponges, and a reef wall pockmarked with caves that are populated by large green turtles, giant grouper and manta rays, and myriad angelfish.

The Outer Islands are perfect for diving

Ask the Angelfish Dive Centre about excursions to the Drop

Doile

In 1873, the French coal steamer *Doile* sank on the reefs to the west of Alphonse. All that remains is the boiler, which sticks out as a marker. Near the boiler there are magical dives revealing gorgeous corals, some the size of a person, where fearless green turtles, stingrays and the giant potato-cod grouper make their homes.

The Drop

The Angelfish Dive Centre on Desroches offers great diving for beginners or more challenging excursions for the experienced. To the south of the island is the Drop, a coral plateau dotted with deep caves and popular with more experienced divers. For optimum conditions and safety, go from October to April when the sea is calm, and always dive with a qualified divemaster.

The dive boat is well equipped and can take a maximum of eight people for unforgettable dives, during which you can gaze at an amazing underwater world of untouched nature. There are single dives and packages of five or ten dives, including night dives. The centre also offers PADI-approved courses and PADI certification. Wetsuits and regulators can be rented in addition to torches and underwater digital cameras, and your pictures can be downloaded onto a CD to take home.

Saint Joseph Atoll

To the north of Desroches, this atoll consists of 13 deserted islets where the diving is first class. The best way to dive is to charter a live-aboard yacht; there are many operators in Mahé and Praslin who can organise this for you.

Getting away from it all

In the Seychelles, you don't have to go very far to find peace and solitude and feel at one with nature. Yet for all the delectable islands, exclusive resorts, beautiful forests and marine parks, there are two special attractions that should not be missed.

Venn's Town/Mission Ruins

Venn's Town, named after the secretary of the London Missionary Society, nestles in the Morne Seychellois National Park on Mahé. Only a short journey from the bustle of the capital, Victoria, a visit here combines nature and history in one hit. Also known as Mission Ruins, this peaceful haven was the site of a missionary school established by the Anglican Church in the 19th century for child slaves rescued by British ships that patrolled the Indian Ocean following the abolition of slavery. The magical forest surrounding the ruins once rang with the laughter of children who, according to Marianne North, the Victorian artist who visited Venn's Town in 1883, 'were very happy and did not puzzle their brains with too much learning'.

View from Mission Ruins

A white-tailed tropicbird

Much of the virgin forest was cleared to make room for the school, and a small farm nearby provided income from coffee, vanilla and coconut plantations. The school closed in 1885, and all that is left are the ruins of the water room and master's house.

Many endemic plants, such as *bwa-d-fer* (*Vateriopsis sechellarum*), are being reintroduced, and the forest has become the natural habitat of birds like the white-tailed tropicbird (*Phaeton lepturus*), a white seabird with two long streaming tails, and the kestrel (*Falco araea*), which swoops down on geckos and insects. At nightfall, you are more likely to hear the low rasping call of the Seychelles scops owl (*Otus insularis*), rather than see this small dark brown bird, which is so rare that no nest has ever been found. Look also for the Capucin tree (*Northea hornei*), named after Marianne North, and endemic palms such as Latanier hauban

(*Roscheria melanochaetes*) and Latanier feuille (*Phoenicophorium borsigianum*).

An avenue of tall sandragon trees (*Pterocarpus indicus*) frames the pathway leading to a timber lodge, giving spectacular views of Mahé's east coast. Planted in the late 19th century, the sandragon, which means 'dragon's blood', oozes red sap when the bark is cut. Overzealous slashing of the bark by curious visitors has sadly affected the sandragons' growth and they are badly diseased, but the trees are a majestic sight and a poignant reminder of the fragility of nature. Other trees include cinnamon, mandarin and breadfruit planted by later settlers, and there are patches of lemon grass which, if rubbed between finger and thumb, give off a pleasant aroma.

6km (4 miles) south along Chemin Sans Souci–Port Glaud road from Victoria. Free car park. Bus: No 14 stops nearby.

Getting away from it all

The unspoilt Aldabra Islands

Aldabra Atoll

The Aldabra group of islands, consisting of Assomption and the atolls of Cosmolédo, Astove and Aldabra itself, is 1,150km (715 miles) southwest of Mahé. Being only 420km (260 miles) northwest of Madagascar, it has nothing in common with the idyllic beaches of the Seychelles. Going there is a humbling, once-in-a-lifetime experience, which leaves you marvelling at the fragility of our environment and the power of nature.

Aldabra is the world's largest raised coral atoll and is made up of four main islands that encircle a lagoon the size of Mahé. Listed as a UNESCO World Heritage Site in 1982 for its unique and fragile ecosystem, it is so far from shipping routes that only a few humans ever land on its shores. In 1964, there were proposals to turn Aldabra into an American military base, but, thanks to international protests from conservationists, the idea was shelved. Today, there is a scientific research station that monitors the many endangered species that proliferate here, in an environment barely touched by the modern world.

Aldabra's jagged coral rocks and wild flat landscapes are the domain of 150,000 giant land tortoises, the largest population in the world, and the habitat of the last remaining flightless bird in the Indian Ocean, the white-throated rail. Aldabra has the second-largest frigate colony in the world, and there are nesting grounds for flamingos and as many as a dozen endemic land birds can be seen. Nesting turtles, rays, sharks and other marine wonders hide in pristine reefs and coral habitats. More than 2,000 turtles lay their eggs on the beaches each year, and, since 2001, the dugong, or sea cow, thought to have vanished forever, has been spotted on four separate occasions in the lagoon.

The logistics of sailing to Aldabra are costly and complicated but not impossible for the determined voyager. You need prior permission from the Seychelles Islands Foundation that manages the islands, and there are strict regulations for visitors. By far the most comfortable way is to look out for the occasional cruise ship, or join an expedition with a specialist travel company (*see below*). Alternatively, you could charter a boat with companies like Angel Fish Yacht Charters or Silhouette Cruises (*see p151*), which take around two weeks to make the return trip, or charter a plane from the Island Development Company in Mahé. This method of travel involves flying to Assomption where you board a specially chartered boat for the three-hour journey to Aldabra.

Eco-warriors can opt for the *Lady Genevieve*, a supply boat from the Island Development Corporation that leaves every two months from Mahé. However, space is limited and you should be prepared to live on a diet of fish and rice for the 12-day voyage. Even then your stay on Aldabra is limited to two hours unless you're one of the very lucky few to find accommodation that is available for the next two months when the supply ship returns.

The other islands of the Aldabra Atoll are off-limits to people, and vessels drop anchor at Picard Island where the research station has just six double rooms normally reserved for scientists. Disembarking into a rubber dinghy tests your nimble-footedness as you wait for the incoming tide to whoosh you through a channel on a roller-coaster ride teeming with hump-backed whales, sharks, turtles and rays and into the spectacular lagoon where the snorkelling is truly out of this world.

1,150km (715 miles) southwest of Mahé. Islands Development Company in Mahé is the only company offering flights to Assomption (Tel: 224 640).
Seychelles Islands Foundation. La Ciotat Building, Mont Fleuri, Victoria, Mahé. Tel: 321 735. www.sif.sc

Watch where you put your feet!

Getting away from it all

When to go

The Seychelles archipelago is situated in the western Indian Ocean between 4 and 10 degrees south of the equator, with Mahé being 1,600km (1,000 miles) east of Africa. The resulting maritime climate provides warm and generally sunny weather year-round without the extreme high temperatures that are experienced in most equatorial countries.

Climate

Temperatures seldom drop below 24°C (75°F) or rise much above 33°C (91°F), with 7½ hours of sunlight every day. Indian Ocean cyclones veer to the southwest of the Seychelles and have never affected the Inner Islands of Mahé, Praslin and La Digue, although cyclonic activity has been known to bring windy weather and grey skies between December and March. Short tropical downpours are common throughout the islands, with more rainfall in January on the Inner Islands, especially on Mahé and Silhouette, than on the outlying coral islands.

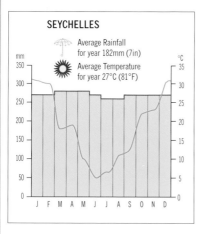

SEYCHELLES

Average Rainfall for year 182mm (7in)

Average Temperature for year 27°C (81°F)

WEATHER CONVERSION CHART

25.4mm = 1 inch

°F = 1.8 × °C + 32

Trade winds

If you want to have more than a beach holiday, then you should be aware that Seychelles' trade winds can have an appreciable effect on what you want to do.

The northwest trade winds from October to March bring generally calm seas and warm tropical weather, with high levels of humidity from March to April.

The southeast trade winds from May to September see drier and cooler weather, most evident on the southeastern coasts, and less humidity.

The sea is always warm and great for sailing, swimming and snorkelling year-round, but avoid July to September when the winds can be very strong, making some beaches dangerous for swimming, and sea crossings quite bumpy. If you visit Praslin, bear in mind that seaweed, brought in on the southeast trade winds, collects on the southern shores between May and October. For keen divers, calmer sea conditions from March to May and September to November provide great underwater visibility of up to 30m (100ft).

Inexperienced sailors may find the choppy conditions uncomfortable in June and July, although surfers and windsurfers will love it. For hiking and walking, you should avoid November to April when paths are slippery and it is also very hot. Serious birdwatchers or part-time twitchers make for the bird islands between May and October, especially those sheltered from trade winds, such as those west of Praslin. The seabird havens of the outer coral islands are best visited in April for the breeding season and May to September for the nesting of sooty terns, and October is generally migration time. The best time for fishing is from October to April.

Beating the crowds

Seychelles is an expensive destination so you shouldn't expect any heavily discounted deals, but prices for accommodation and flights tend to drop slightly from late October through to November, especially in budget, mid-range and self-catering properties. If you plan to go during these times, it's best to book well ahead as places fill up fast. Many of the larger hotels charge a supplement from mid-December to the end of January, Easter and August.

Dramatic clouds in December

Getting around

Bus services run by Seychelles Transport Company (STC) operate only on Mahé and Praslin, ferries operate between Mahé, Praslin and La Digue, and you can fly to most islands or charter your own boat. If you want to do your own thing once you arrive on Mahé or the Inner Islands, then it is better to hire a car. Some Inner and all the Outer Islands have no bus service or car-hire facilities, and the only way of getting around is by foot or bicycle.

By bus

In theory, you could explore Mahé and Praslin by bus at a fixed SR7 fare for any distance travelled, but you need to equate this with the vagaries of the bus timetable, which is more geared to local use rather than tourists' needs. Even though bus timetables are published, drivers rarely keep to them and it's not unusual to be waiting for what seems

Buses are cheap, but not suitable for everyone

all day for the bus. Timetables are available from hotels and the main bus terminus in Palm Street, Victoria. Queues are orderly and you pay the fare on board. Having the right change helps. Buses are not the ideal method of travel for people with disabilities or very young children since journeys can be slow or lightning fast depending on the whims of the driver, and accidents are common, especially on narrow roads. Buses operate between 6am and 7pm.

By air

Flights with the national airline Air Seychelles from Mahé domestic terminal go to the Inner Islands of Praslin, Bird, Denis and Frégate and to the Outer Island of Desroches via Alphonse. Check-in time is 30 minutes before departure and a 15kg (33lb) baggage limit applies.

Helicopter Seychelles flies to the private islands of Bird, Denis, Cousine, Félicité, Frégate, North and Silhouette. In Mahé, there are helipads at the Banyan Tree Resort and the islands of Cerf, Ronde and Sainte Anne. On Praslin, there are helipads at Lemuria Resort, Côte d'Or and Château des Feuilles Hotels and on La Digue.

Another way of taking in the beauty of the islands is to take a scenic flight over Sainte Anne National Marine Park. Prices start from €380 for a 15-minute flip but flights can last up to one hour. For all helicopter flights and transfers, you should keep baggage to a maximum of 10kg (22lb).

Air Seychelles flies to most of the Inner and some Outer Islands

Helicopter Seychelles. PO Box 595, Victoria. Tel: 385 863. Fax: 373 055. Email: info@helicopterseychelles.sc. www.helicopterseychelles.com. Open: 8am–6pm.

By car

Most Seychellois drive quite sedately, although some bus drivers treat the narrow winding roads like racetracks and you should always give buses a wide berth. Roads are generally in good condition, but most are unlit at night. The speed limit is 40kph (25mph) in town, 60kph (37mph) outside town and 65kph (40mph) on the dual carriageway between Victoria and the airport. On Praslin, the speed limit is 40kph (25mph). There is only one set of traffic lights in Victoria, and during rush hours traffic can get quite heavy. so avoid these times if you can. Elsewhere driving is pleasurable and safe.

Car hire

Expect to pay from €50 a day for basic car hire, but you should check that this includes insurance and tax. To hire a car you must be over 21 and have a valid international licence or EU driver's licence. Vehicles are driven on the left-hand side of the road. If you have an accident, inform the hirer immediately. There are plenty of car-hire companies at Mahé airport.

Tropicar. Tel: 373 336.
Email: tropicar@Seychelles.net
Thrifty Car Rentals. Coral Strand Hotel, Beau Vallon. Tel: 247 052.
Cozy Car Hire. Tel: 266 409.
Viva. Tel: 247 500.
www.car-rental-seychelles.com

By ferry

Scheduled ferry services to Praslin on the *Cat Cocos*, a high-speed catamaran, are operated by **Cat Cocos Inter Island Boats** (*Port Victoria, Mahé. Tel: 297 160. Email: reservation@catcocos.com; www. catcocos.com*) and **Baie Sainte Anne** (*Praslin. Tel: 232 616*). Departures from Mahé are Mon–Sat at 7.30am and 4pm, return 9am and 5.30pm, and Sunday at 10.30am and 4.30pm, return 3pm and 6pm. The journey takes 45 minutes.

Ferries from Praslin with the **Inter Island Ferry** (*Tel: 232 329*) provide regular connections with La Digue, and some are timed to link up with passengers arriving or departing from Praslin for Mahé. The journey time is 30 minutes. Tickets can be bought on the quaysides at Praslin and La Digue, or ask your hotel or tour operator to arrange this for you. All fares are payable in foreign currency.

By organised tour

Many travel agents organise tours by coach or private car with a driver on

The catamaran ferry in Victoria

Yachts at Praslin

Mahé and Praslin or by taxi on La Digue. The following companies are all based in Mahé and can arrange personalised itineraries and accommodation. They also have desks at most hotels and representatives at the domestic and international air terminals, and at ferry ports.
7 Degrees South. Tel: 292 800.
Creole Travel Services. Tel: 297 000.
Masons Travel. Tel: 288 888.

By taxi

There are taxis on Mahé, Praslin and a handful on La Digue. Some taxis have stands outside hotels, and the best way of hiring one is through the receptionist. Although taxis are metered, they are rarely used so you should always fix a price before accepting a ride. As a guideline, expect

to pay €14 from the airport to Victoria plus extra for baggage, and €10 for a return journey from Beau Vallon to Victoria. Drivers do not expect to be tipped. Taxi fares are slightly higher in Praslin, and with so few in La Digue you should book well ahead.

By yacht charter

International charter and Seychellois-owned companies have a wide range of sail and powered catamarans, yachts and monohulls, with or without crew. The price includes accommodation in well-appointed cabins, all meals, soft drinks, facilities for diving, snorkelling, swimming and some land excursions. Details of operators can be obtained from the official Seychelles website on *www.seychelles.travel*

Accommodation

Seychelles is one of the world's most expensive destinations, but if money is no object and you yearn for an island to call your own, there are 18 to choose from. These islands, known as 'one resort one island' destinations, are privately owned and, apart from Sainte Anne Island Resort with over 80 villas, cater for a very small number of guests, making it not unusual to bid good morning to the likes of royalty, film stars, footballers and captains of industry on your way to breakfast.

All of these islands are in beautiful locations, the accommodation is luxuriously appointed, and the cuisine is a work of art prepared by master chefs. All come at a price, but they are built to very high standards and are managed by expatriate Europeans and locally employed English-speaking staff.

There are very few large hotels. By Seychellois standards, a hotel is large if it has more than 25 rooms. The small hotels, although not necessarily cheaper, are very well appointed and include air conditioning, private terrace, TV and IDD telephones, while others appeal to those seeking a home-from-home niche. Accommodation is not officially star-rated as in European countries, but hotels described in travel brochures as '5-star' most certainly live up to this category.

Accommodation in mid-range hotels is also of a high standard with efficient and welcoming staff. In some of the less grand hotels there is a worn 1960s feel in the public areas, although refurbishment programmes are in hand. There may not be so many restaurants to choose from, the swimming pool may be smaller, the hotel set in less spacious grounds and you're unlikely to have room service. However, you will find that they occupy pleasant beach locations, the rooms are comfortable, and hairdryers, shaving points, IDD telephones, air conditioning, tea- and coffee-making facilities and TV come as standard. You may also get Internet access. Some of the larger mid-range hotels have extra facilities, such as babysitting services and separate children's pools.

Budget options may appear to be thin on the ground and, mindful of the expense involved in staying in the Seychelles, the tourism authorities are promoting more affordable accommodation under the 'Seychelles Secrets' branding scheme. The properties are usually family-run and owned, and can be small hotels, guesthouses and self-catering units located by the sea or very close to it. Quite often they are near bus stops and shops, and staying in this type of accommodation is a great way to get close to the people. Breakfast is usually included in the price, and owners can prepare an evening meal. With an emphasis on cleanliness, comfort, décor and value for money, this accommodation is very popular with both Seychellois and overseas visitors so it's wise to book well ahead by telephone or email (*visit www.seychellessecrets.com*).

Another option is to charter a boat and live aboard for the duration of your holiday. The cost of the charter can be split among a group, making chartering less expensive than if you were to go it alone (*see p100*).

There are no campsites in the Seychelles – camping is not allowed.

Acajou hotel in Praslin, set in lush gardens

Accommodation

Food and drink

Seychellois cuisine is quite different to the Creole cuisine you might encounter in other parts of the world. It tends to be lighter, less fiery and infinitely more fish-based than the Creole cuisine of, say, the Caribbean or Mauritius. Due to the Seychelles' remoteness, cooks have had to rely on their ingenuity to produce creative and colourful cuisine. With an ocean teeming with fish, gardens bursting with spices and fruit trees, and influences from all the great continents, visitors will not be disappointed with the local fare.

In the 18th century, French settlers brought their culinary skills to the Seychelles and combined them with whatever fish was to hand. African slaves added *manioc* (cassava), sweet potato and banana to the cooking pot, while nearest island neighbours Réunion and Madagascar provided vanilla, ginger and garlic. Indian and later Chinese merchants jazzed things up with spices from the east, while the British grew yet more essential ingredients, the humble coconut and cinnamon. The result is that today's cuisine is a combination of French savoir-faire and Asian bite, sprinkled with a little British tradition.

The sea has always been a natural larder for the Seychellois, yielding enough fish to feed a nation and the thousands of tourists who arrive each year. Fishermen go out twice a day, and you need only stroll along Beau Vallon beach to see sizeable catches of fat mackerel, *zob* (snapper), *karang* (trevally), parrotfish and bonito, which

are quickly sold to local housewives and restaurateurs.

Fish in all its forms is the number one favourite with all Seychellois. They eat it fried, grilled, curried, wrapped in a banana leaf and baked, and it even turns up as British-style battered fish and chips. On restaurant menus you'll find the *bourzwa* (red snapper), highly prized and priced in Europe, yet affordable and plentiful in the Seychelles. The *bourzwa* is often served whole and grilled and, depending on the whims of the cook, can be spiked with ginger, garlic and the red-hot chilli.

You'll also find delicious curries masquerading as *caris masala* and saffron-flavoured rice as *pulao*, both palate-titillating imports from India, and Gallic-inspired grilled swordfish marinated in oil and lime. For a different take on swordfish, try it as *chatini*, a type of chutney made by grating the flesh with turmeric, garlic and a sour fruit called *bilimbi*, and served as an accompaniment to a traditional Creole meal.

A Creole meal is typically a large whole fish served up in all its glory on a platter accompanied by smaller dishes of fish, chicken, pork or goat curry with a selection of vegetables that may include deep-fried aubergines, mashed pumpkin or lentils, and greens called *bredes*. It's rare to have a starter, but if you do you will probably have *palmis*, a salad made from the grated shoots of the coconut palm and dressed with lime juice and oil. All the dishes arrive together and you simply tuck in to whatever you fancy. Vegetarians are well catered for too as vegetable oil, as opposed to animal fat, is normally used in cooking. Vegetables include the gut-busting breadfruit, which can come as crispy chips or steamed or boiled whole and cut into slices, topped with a knob of butter.

The colonial architecture of the Marie Antoinette Restaurant, Victoria

Some curries may be too hot for Europeans, but if you prefer them mild go for one that includes *kari koko* (coconut milk). Coconut milk is used in the fabulously tender octopus curry, known as *kari koko zourit*, and if it's too mild you can always spike it with a fiery chilli sauce.

A good indicator of the popularity of a restaurant is the number of people using it, and there are several in Victoria worth trying. They tend to get very busy at lunch time as locals tuck into pizzas and pastas, baguettes and sandwiches, chicken and chips, and the ubiquitous fish dishes. Many office workers prefer fast food in the form of chicken or meat curries, grilled fish, and vegetable offerings served up in polystyrene containers from numerous takeaways in the streets near the market. If you're in a hurry and don't mind eating on the hoof, these meals are excellent value for money. Outside Victoria there are restaurants specialising in seafood, Creole, Italian, Indian and French cuisine.

Many hotel restaurants have theme buffet evenings that give you an opportunity to try a whole range of food from the Seychelles and beyond, while dining à la carte in the more exclusive hideaways will introduce you to cuisine with a fine French twist, but whatever you do leave room for the *petits fours*. Desserts include ice creams flavoured with *sitronel* (citronella) or cinnamon and may be served with fresh fruit. If you're into all things sweet, look out for *ladob*, a filling confection made from breadfruit, banana or sweet potato, and cooked with coconut milk.

Exotic produce on the menu at the Denis Island Resort

A buffet at the Boat House Restaurant, Beau Vallon

Nearly all foodstuffs are imported, and eating out or indeed buying your own can be very expensive. The market in Victoria groans with fish, yet the vegetable and fruit stalls are not piled high with produce as you might expect but laid out in small plastic bags. In villages, you'll find helpful corner shops selling basics in small quantities, and these are handy places to stock up if you're self-catering or organising your own picnic. Many Seychellois are self-sufficient, although this is changing, especially in northern Mahé where new housing and smaller gardens mean less space to grow fruit and vegetables. Eating in restaurants or dining in hotels is reserved for special occasions, and most are happy to spend the day having a barbecue or picnic *en famille* on the beach.

Smoking is banned inside most restaurants and other enclosed public areas and workplaces, although there are some outdoor areas where you can light up. Many hotel restaurants expect you to dress properly for dinner, which basically means that shorts and T-shirts are out.

There are two locally produced beers, Seybrew and Eku, and tropical fruits like passion fruit, pawpaw and mango turn up in refreshing drinks. After a meal try *sitronel*, made from lemon grass, as an aid to digestion. For the local firewater there is *kalou* and *baka* and the highly lethal *lapire*, all guaranteed to make you see double.

Entertainment

Being an island nation spread over so many thousands of kilometres of ocean, there is very little in the way of nightlife, café culture or highbrow entertainment in the Seychelles. However, that's not to say there is nothing to while away the sunny days and balmy evenings, but it is generally known that the Seychellois people rise with the sun and go to bed early, and many visitors find that they too are soon lulled into a similar routine.

There is limited nightlife on Mahé or Praslin, and if you're staying elsewhere what nightlife there is usually revolves around the hotels. The best way to find out what's on is at the tourist office at Victoria or Beau Vallon, or speak to your hotel receptionist.

Casinos

If you want to gamble there are several casinos where you can play blackjack, poker or roulette or try your luck on the gaming machines. Some casinos have a restaurant and arrangements with hotels, which can supply free transport there and back. The dress code is smart casual.

Cinema

There are two cinemas in Mahé showing English films.

Dance

The traditional dance of the Seychelles is the *moutya*, which has its roots in slavery. The dance was a form of

escapism from the harshness of captivity, but today young Seychellois express joy rather than the suffering of their ancestors and some have formed themselves into groups and are only too keen to share their cultural heritage with visitors. Look out for performers,

The Pirates Arms in Victoria has live music

The grand exterior of Praslin casino

on Wednesday afternoons, as the sun goes down on the beach at Beau Vallon, and on Sundays from around 6pm onwards, or local musician Keven Valentin, who performs at Kaz Kreole restaurant at weekends. If you are in the Seychelles in October, you should not miss the Festival Kreol (*see p21*), a week-long festival of music, culture, food and street parties and lots of entertainment specially put on at many hotels.

Your hotel may provide theme buffet evenings but you are more likely to be serenaded by crooning local musicians. Sometimes there may be a *sega* dance show. The *sega*, a dance common to the western Indian Ocean islands, shares its origins with the *moutya* and involves a lot of feet-shuffling and swaying of hips to an accompaniment of electric guitars and drums, and a singer recounting lyrics of simple daily events. Depending

on the enthusiasm of the audience, you may be invited to join in.

Nightlife

The best place for nightlife outside of the hotels in Mahé is Beau Vallon, although even here it is very low-key with only a few bars and restaurants. The most animated is The Boat House Restaurant (*see p148*), which is packed every night with tourists and locals tucking into the fixed-price Creole buffet. The Pirates Arms (*see p150*) in Victoria has a bar and restaurant and is a popular nightspot with visitors and islanders who come to listen to musicians playing modern and traditional Seychellois music.

There are no nightclubs as such, but you could try the lively discotheques in Mahé and Praslin. They normally open at 10pm and close at around 4am or when the last person leaves.

Seychellois art

Seychellois art has taken off in leaps and bounds in recent years in response to an increase in tourism. Away from the beaches there are many studios and galleries displaying work by local artists. Several overseas artists have also settled in the Seychelles, inspired by the beauty of the sea and land. Work can be commissioned or purchased direct from these artists, but be prepared for high prices. If you can't visit the studios, Kenwyn House in Victoria and Thoughts at Bel Air Road (*see p129*) also display and sell works by local artists.

Antonio Filippin Sculpture Studio

This Italian sculptor settled in the Seychelles in 1992 and works in a simple thatched studio in the village of Baie Lazare. All his creations are made from coral and wood and other natural materials, which he skilfully turns into works of art.

Anse Gouvernement, Baie Lazare, Mahé. Tel: 510 977. Fax: 361 812. Email: arc@seychelles.sc. Open: Mon–Sat 10am–5pm.

Barbara Jenson Studio

Just past the main entrance of La Digue Island Lodge, this studio is home to a selection of tropical-inspired watercolour and acrylic paintings. Barbara Jenson also draws in pencil and charcoal and specialises in marbled and hand-coloured papers and fabrics.

Street art in Victoria

Anse Réunion, La Digue. Tel: 234 406.
Fax: 234 422.
Email: jenson@seychelles.net.
www.barbarajensonstudio.com
Open: Mon–Sat 9am–5pm.

Colbert Nourrice Studio

A talented young Seychellois artist, specialising in abstract narratives on canvas using signs and symbols that are reminiscent of Egyptian hieroglyphics, is also famous for his symbolic paintings of everyday life.
Domaine de Val des Près, Au Cap, Mahé. Tel: 375 952. Fax: 376 118.
Email: colbertnourrice@seychelles.sc.
Open: Mon–Sat 9am–5pm.

George Camille Art Gallery

Capturing the colour and spirit of Creole life, George Camille works in various media including etching, acrylic and relief collage. His work has been exhibited in major European capitals and he has studios in Praslin and La Digue.
Kaz Zanana, Revolution Avenue, Victoria, Mahé. Tel: 324 150.
Fax: 344 334. www.georgecamille.sc.
Open: Mon–Fri 9am–5pm,
Sat 9am–1pm.

Kreasyon Artist Studio

Seychellois artist Egbert Marday works in a studio just outside Victoria. Here, you'll find a colourful range of acrylics, oils, collage and mixed media work. Look out too for his unusual sculptures made from wood, plaster of Paris, metal, clay and resin.
La Misère Road, Mahé. Tel/fax: 378 456. Email: emarday@seychelles.net.
Open: Mon–Sat 10am–6pm, Sun by appointment.

Michael Adams Studio

At Anse aux Poules Bleues, it's worth calling in at Michael Adams' studio to marvel at his brilliant silk-screen prints. This gentle, animal-loving, Malaysian-born British artist came to the Seychelles in 1972 and is renowned for his vivid paintings of village life and luscious forests. The small studio is crammed with prints and he is delighted to show you around.
Anse aux Poules Bleues. Tel: 361 006.
Fax: 361 200. Email: adams@ seychelles.net. www. michaeladamsart.com.
Open: Mon–Fri 10am–4pm.

Tom Bowers Sculpting Studio

This London-born artist works in a studio nestling in a valley near Anse à la Mouche. His limited editions of fine sculptures of local people are made from resin and cast in bronze.
Santa Maria, Anse à la Mouche.
Tel: 371 518. Fax: 371 075.
Email: artworks@seychelles.net.
Open: Mon–Sat 9am–5.30pm.

Shopping

There is not a lot on offer in the way of traditional Seychellois handicrafts or souvenirs apart from items made from the ubiquitous coconut. However, with an increase in tourism craftworkers are beginning to produce souvenirs. Choosing something to take home can be time-consuming, simply because of the lack of specialist shops, but if you look hard enough you may find some unusual gifts.

WHAT TO BUY

It's worth buying the aromatic soaps and toiletries produced from local essential oils, hand-printed beachwear, baskets, and bags or packets of tea and spices as a memento of your visit. At the luxury end, although hardly Seychellois, are South African diamonds and precious gems, fine art

Shopping for *pareos*, Mahé

and designer label items, such as Melvil & Moon luggage and genuine Panama hats.

Typical of the Seychelles are colourful paintings and prints that can be bought direct from local artists. Names to look out for are Michael Adams, Egbert Marday, Colbert Nourrice and work by Barbara Jensen (*see pp126–7*). Also stained-glass mobiles by Les and Sharon Masterson featuring Seychellois birds, and fish or bronze sculptures by Tom Bowers (*see p127*).

The *coco de mer* (*see pp62–3*) may make an unusual centrepiece for your home. These massive nuts are sold in most tourist shops and come highly polished or in their natural state. Do make sure that your purchase is sold with an export certificate otherwise you will have trouble at customs when leaving the country, and remember that they are extremely heavy. You can also buy fake ones made from wood, or tiny nuts shaped into keyrings.

WHERE TO BUY

Mahé, particularly the capital, Victoria, is the best place for shopping. If you're staying elsewhere, you'll find a limited range of expensive items in hotel boutiques. Prices are fixed in shops but bargaining with street traders may yield a tiny discount. Bear in mind that even in Mahé prices are higher than those in Europe, and you are unlikely to come across any bargains.

Camion Hall in Victoria's Albert Street is a small arcade of souvenir shops and bookshops, and there are more tourist kiosks lining Fiennes Esplanade off Francis Rachael Street. The streets around the market and indeed inside the market are also good places for browsing, and you may come across snazzy T-shirts and dresses, vanilla pods, cinnamon and curry spices, unusual woodcarvings of tortoises or even original jewellery crafted from beads and shells.

Local brew, Coco d'Amour

Mahé
Craft Village
Hand-painted glass, candles, woven mats, dolls and scented soaps and perfumes.
Domaine de Val des Près, Anse aux Pins.
Tel: 376 100. Open: 9.30am–5.30pm.
Free admission.

Kenwyn House
Memorabilia, diamonds, precious gems and fine art.
Francis Rachel Street, Victoria.
Tel: 224 440. www.kenwynhouse.com

Memorabilia
Books, maps, souvenirs, coconut trinkets, jewellery.
Rue de la Revolution, Victoria.
Tel: 321 190.

Pineapple Studios
Imported *pareos* (sarongs) and T-shirts with hand-printed Seychelles emblems. Also scented soaps, toiletries and *coco de mer* souvenirs.
Anse aux Poules Bleues. Tel: 361 230.
Fax: 361 463.

Thoughts
Stained glass, work by local artists, woven crafts.
Bel Air Road, Mahé. Tel: 321 254.

Sport and leisure

The year-round good weather is the biggest draw for visitors to the Seychelles, and with an ocean to explore and lush landscapes to discover, there's no shortage of activities providing both relaxation and exercise for amateurs and professionals alike.

Birdwatching

The Seychelles is a year-round bird-watchers' paradise. You have every chance of spotting rare endemic birds, unusual migrants and huge colonies of seabirds provided you go at the right time and to the right place. Local tour operators can organise special bird-watching tours that feature Praslin and Bird, and the nature reserve islands of Cousin and Aride, or you can book through a specialist tour operator in your home country.

You need not look far for the more common species to the Seychelles, such as the blue pigeon, the cave swiftlet, the bulbul and sunbird. If birdwatching takes a hold on you, it's useful to invest in a laminated identification card published by the Island Conservation Society and available in bookshops, which shows pictures of all the land, sea and shore birds found in the Seychelles.

Cruising

See pp100–101.

Cycling

Cycling is a fun way of exploring many of the islands and, as you get further away from Mahé, it is often the only means of getting around. On islands where there is only one resort, such as Desroches, a bicycle is provided free and left outside your villa. On La Digue, with its flat terrain and absence of traffic, there is no end of bicycles for hire. Some bicycles are better than others, and you should always check the brakes before setting off.

Diving

Diving is hugely popular and there are myriad dive sites to explore throughout the Seychelles. There are six dive sites alone near Frégate Island, the most popular being Lion Rock where rock formations have created ideal conditions for young reef sharks. Dive centres are found on the beaches and most are members of the Association of Professional Divers Seychelles and comply with strict safety regulations.

The boats are well equipped and all diving gear is provided. There are also a number of boat-based operators that undertake longer excursions.

If you're a beginner there are dive schools offering internationally recognised PADI courses. These courses last for four days, starting off in the hotel swimming pool or shallow waters and with tutorial sessions to learn the basic skills. You then undertake dives in limited depths under supervision, which entitles you to the PADI Scuba Diver Certificate. If you persevere over the next two days and complete your training successfully, you will receive the PADI Open Water Dive Certificate entitling you to dive anywhere in the world.

Fishing

Clear, sandy shallows and deep waters beyond the reef teeming with marine life make fishing the number one sport in the Seychelles. Whether it's big-game fishing, fly-fishing, bone fishing, tag and release or trawling, you don't have to go very far to return with a catch. The country is the holder of 12 International Game Fishing Awards, which include world records for Pacific bonito and dogtooth tuna. The Seychelles Bank to the north of Denis Island, where the ocean floor plunges hundreds of metres, teems with barracuda and shark, while the flats on Saint François and Alphonse Islands rank among the best in the world for fly fishing. Many operators specialise in

game fishing and can tailor an itinerary, providing crew and all equipment. Trips can be a half day, full day or several days depending on your wishes, and all equipment is provided.

For details of operators contact the Marine Charter Association, Victoria Harbour. Tel: 322 126. Open: 8am–noon, 1–4pm.

Golf

Although the Seychelles is hardly an internationally recognised golfing

A dramatic setting for the Lemuria Resort golf course

destination, the challenging 18-hole course at the Lemuria Resort in Praslin (*see p152*), surrounded by ponds and hills and with a magnificent viewpoint of the satellite islands from the 15th tee, may appeal to golfers. It is open to non-residents but you should book beforehand. You can find a nine-hole golf course at the Reef Golf Club opposite the former Reef Hotel just south of the airport. This golf course is in an old coconut plantation and some say the trees are too close for comfort, but the staff are helpful and there is no need to book except on Saturdays when local competitions are held.

Hiking

There are nine walks and trails in the Morne Seychellois National Park, and booklets describing the trails can be obtained from the kiosk in the Botanical Gardens. From coastal routes and mountain summits to flat and steep terrain, they are a wonderful way of exploring the hinterland and the flora and fauna. For the low-graded walks it's safe to go without a guide, but for the

Brush up on your sailing skills, or hire a guide

A gentle woodland walk on Desroches Island

medium- and high-graded walks you should hire a guide. You can get details of qualified guides from the tourist office. Some walks, like the coastal walk from Danzilles to Grande Anse, take a few hours to complete depending on your ability, but for others you should allow between a half and a full day.

The best time to go hiking is during the cooler months between June and September, but always check weather conditions before you set off as trails can get very slippery if it rains. Let someone know of your whereabouts if you go alone, and remember that it gets dark by about 6.30pm. Wear good hiking shoes or boots, always carry water and food with you, don't stray from the marked paths alone, never drink water from mountain streams, and take all your litter home.

Botanical Gardens. Mont Fleuri Road, Victoria. Tel: 670 500. Open: 8am–5pm.

Horse riding

The Utegangar Riding Centre on Mahé (*see p147*) is the only riding centre on the island and caters for beginners and the experienced. Rides on Arab horses range from one hour to half a day, and take you along the nearby beaches of Anse Cimetière, Anse Barbarons and Grande Anse, and depend on the tide. There are mountain, forest and river trails for the more experienced. Helmets, saddles and tack are all supplied and it's best to wear long trousers rather than shorts. You should make a reservation at least one day ahead. Horses can also be hired at L'Union Estate on La Digue (*see p155*).

Children

The Seychelles are not just for the sporty and romantic but cater well for children too, especially if they are curious about the natural world. Given the right sense of direction, enthusiasm and imagination, a family holiday in the Seychelles is much more than fun in the sun, although that plays a large part in the itinerary. It's a good idea to tell children from the outset that although there are no amusement arcades or fairgrounds, there are plenty of other exciting opportunities.

If you're on a budget and all the little ones need is pure beach, then you can't go wrong with a stay at Coral Strand Hotel at Beau Vallon (*see p148*), where the sea is usually calm and lifeguards watch year-round. A day out could include a trip to Victoria's Botanical Gardens to see the giant tortoises (*see pp29–30*), perhaps followed by a visit to the Natural History Museum (*see p31*) where interactive kiosks play the different calls of birdsong. Giant tortoises are a feature of the Seychelles, and you'll find many of these specimens kept as pets in people's gardens or roaming in the grounds of hotels. If your kids are budding David Attenboroughs, look out for *The Tortoise Who Thought He Was a Dodo* in Victoria's bookshops. This is a book for children that recounts the rediscovery of the species and is written by resident tortoise expert Ron Gerlach.

On Côte d'Or beach on Praslin's north coast, shallow waters make it perfectly safe for children. Should they get bored and fancy stretching their legs, a walk in the Vallée de Mai (*see pp64–5*) is sure to awaken their senses to nature as they hunt for endemic snails, identify different birds and seek

Don't worry, palm spiders won't bite!

A day at the beach will keep the little ones amused

out harmless palm spiders spinning webs between tall *coco de mer* palms. Although there are clearly marked paths, some of the steps are uneven and may not be suitable for very small children.

Lemuria Resort (*see p152*), also on Praslin, is well suited for children, with apartment-style suites linked by an external lobby and access to spacious gardens and the beach. For state-of-the-art accommodation, go for the private pool villas that consist of two huge en-suite bedrooms overlooking a sunken dining area, and which come with a villa master to tend to all needs. There is also a Turtle Club for children, with a computer and play area positioned at a decent distance away from those seeking romance and tranquillity.

If the kids like cycling, consider a holiday on La Digue (*see pp74–7*). With barely any traffic, apart from ox-carts and the odd taxi or pickup truck, you can hire special children and adult bikes from many operators, but always check the brakes before setting off.

Mini-clubs are a relative newcomer to the Seychelles, but most hotels can provide babysitters, provided they are given sufficient notice. When choosing a hotel, bear in mind that some do not accept children under 12 and check with your travel agent. Children are welcome in restaurants everywhere and many establishments provide special meals. Baby products, such as nappies and tinned food, are available but you may not always find a brand from home.

Essentials

Arriving in the Seychelles
By air
Air Seychelles (HM) flies direct from London (Heathrow and Gatwick), Paris, Rome, Milan, Chennai, Mauritius, Singapore, Cape Town and Johannesburg. Other major carriers are Etihad and Emirates from Dubai, Kenya Airways, Condor and Air Austral. All visitors arrive at **Mahé International Airport** (*Tel: 384 400*) 10km (6 miles) south of the capital, Victoria. There is a foreign exchange facility outside the arrivals terminal, car-hire desks, a tour operator kiosk for greeting incoming visitors, and taxi stands. The taxi fare to the centre of Victoria is €14 plus extra for luggage, or at night. There is a public bus service to Victoria and the stop is right outside the airport. The fare is SR7 and is suitable only if you don't have a lot of luggage.

By sea
Port Victoria on Mahé is the only official port of entry. If arriving on a cruise ship, the operator will have completed formalities. Private yachters must comply with customs, health, immigration and port and security formalities in person at Port Victoria, with a valid outward clearance certificate from their last port of call.

Customs
You are allowed to import free of tax 2 litres of spirits and 2 litres of wine, 200 cigarettes or 250g of tobacco and 200ml of perfume or eau de toilette.

Arrivals at Praslin airport

Departing

There is no departure tax and any additional taxes are included in the cost of your air ticket. Private yachters must have an exit clearance from customs.

Electricity

The power supply in the Seychelles is 220 volts. The UK three-pin square plug is standard throughout the islands. Hotels can normally supply adaptors for foreign appliances, but if in doubt take your own. Power cuts on the Inner Islands are rare. On the Outer Islands generators supply electricity.

Shops in the Seychelles have shorter opening hours than those in the UK

Money

The Seychelles rupee (SR) is divided into 100 cents. Notes consist of SR10, SR25, SR50, SR100 and SR500. Coins come in denominations of 5 cents, 10 cents, 25 cents, SR1 and SR5.

Seychelles has a fluctuating currency, and you should avoid changing too much currency at once. On 1 November 2008, the Government of Seychelles removed foreign currency restrictions that required visitors to pay for accommodation and other services in hard currency, as part of its economic reform programme. Non-residents can now pay for goods and services, including car hire, transfers and entrance fees, in either Seychelles rupees or hard currency such as sterling, US dollars or euros.

A black market for currency is all too evident, especially on Mahé's Beau Vallon beach where you will be asked with amazing regularity if you want to change any spare dollars, euros or pounds. Although the authorities turn a blind eye to this illegal practice, do bear in mind that if somebody does report you there are severe penalties.

ATMs, credit and debit cards

ATMs (cashpoint machines) are widely available, and instructions are given in English. Most restaurants and shops outside hotels accept major credit cards, such as MasterCard and Visa, but always check beforehand.

Opening hours

Offices are open Monday to Friday 8am–4pm and some on Saturday from 8am–noon. Banks are open Monday to Friday 8.30am–2pm and Saturday 8.30–11am. Shops are open Monday to Friday 8am–5pm and Saturday 8am–noon.

Passports and visas

Visitors must be in possession of a valid passport, a return air ticket, proof of accommodation, and sufficient funds for the duration of their stay. No visas are necessary from any country, but you will be issued with a 30-day Visitors' Entry Permit that you should keep with you at all times and present to immigration when you leave.

Pharmacies

The only pharmacy in Seychelles is: **Behram's**, *Victoria Arcade, Mahé. Tel: 225 559. Open: Mon–Fri 8.15am–1pm & 2–5.15pm.*

Prescription medicine may be available at dispensaries (*Open: Mon–Fri 8am–6pm, Sat–Sun 8am–noon*) at the following government hospitals:
Victoria Hospital. *Tel: 388 000.*
Baie Sainte Anne Hospital, *Baie Sainte Anne, Praslin. Tel 232 333.*
Logan Hospital Dispensary, *La Passe, La Digue. Tel: 234 255.*

Post

The main post office in Mahé is on Independence Avenue, Victoria, with sub-offices on Praslin and La Digue. Post offices are open Monday to Friday 8am–4pm and Saturday 8am–noon. It costs SR7 to send a 20g air letter to Europe, Australia and Asia, SR8 to America, and SR7 to send a postcard to anywhere in the world. You can find postboxes outside police stations. Hotels also sell stamps and can post your mail.

Public holidays

1 and 2 Jan – New Year
Apr (dates vary) – Good Friday, Easter Day
1 May – Labour Day
5 June – Liberation Day
10 June – Corpus Christi
18 June – National Day
29 June – Independence Day
15 Aug – Assomption Day
1 Nov – All Saints' Day
8 Dec – Immaculate Conception
25 Dec – Christmas

Suggested reading

If you're interested in learning more about the culture and country, there are many books that can be bought in local shops or direct from the authors.

Books: Fiction
Voices by Glynn Burridge
A collection of short stories mostly based in the Amirantes.
The Tortoise Who Thought He Was a Dodo by Ron Gerlach
Amusing book written for children about the tortoise, with illustrations.
Books: Non-fiction
Silhouette – Nature's Island by Gill, Justin and Ron Gerlach
This is a handy reference book on flora and fauna if visiting Silhouette Island, and includes some background history.
Famous Tortoises by Justin Gerlach
As its title suggests, this is an account of famous tortoises.
A Grain of Sand by Brendon Grimshaw
Highly readable and amusing account

by former newspaperman about his experiences of living on Moyenne Island.
Rivals in Eden by William McAteer
A historic account of rivalry between the French and British for control of the sea route to India.

Birds of Seychelles by Adrian Skerrett
A unique guide to all the birds on the Seychelles.
Beyond the Reefs by William Travis
This is a collection of stories by a former pilot who explored the Outer Islands.

The Brown Noddy can be seen year round in the Seychelles

Media

The Nation (*www.nation.sc*) and *The People* (*www.thepeople.sc*) are published daily and contain articles in English, French and Creole. Both papers can be read online. Broadcasts in English, French and Creole are made on the government-owned Radio Seychelles and private Paradise FM Radio. CNN and BBC news programmes are shown on the Seychelles Broadcasting Corporation (SBC), while satellite TV offers a variety of channels.

Tax

There is a 10 per cent VAT charge on restaurants and hotel bills.

Telephones

The international dialling code for Seychelles is 248. You can make international calls and send faxes from virtually any fixed landline in the Seychelles, and even the Outer Islands have satellite communications. Either way you can expect high charges, particularly if calling from your hotel. You can make cheaper international calls at payphones using a pre-purchased phonecard available from shops everywhere.

If you have a mobile phone, the easiest way to keep in touch is to replace your SIM card with a local one. Cable & Wireless and Airtel both have offices in Mahé, Praslin and La Digue and sell pre-paid SR100 starter packs. Top-up cards are available from outlets displaying their logos.

Internet

Many hotels have Internet connections either located in a dedicated section or direct from your room, and there are Internet cafés in Mahé and Praslin. If you have a Wi-Fi enabled laptop, you can hook into a Wi-Fi hotspot. There is one at Mahé International Airport, for which you have to pay, but free Wi-Fi connection for guests is available at the Hilton Seychelles and Fisherman's Cove and an increasing number of hotels on Mahé.

Time

Seychelles is four hours ahead of GMT. This means that when it is noon in the Seychelles, it is 8am in London, 3am in New York, 4am in Montreal, 8pm in Sydney, 9pm in Wellington and 10am in Cape Town.

Toilets

Public toilets are clean, most are equipped with toilet paper, washbasins and/or hand dryer, and are regularly maintained. In Victoria, there are free public toilets in the car park opposite the cathedral, at the market and a pay toilet (SR1) in the port area. Those belonging to restaurants are usually shared with other shops and kept under lock and key.

Tourist office

There is a newly opened Seychelles Tourist Office in London.
73 Newman Street, London W1T 3EJ.
Tel: 0207 636 7954.

Email: seychelles@uksto.co.uk.
www.seychelles.travel

Travellers with disabilities

Access to hotels located on hillsides involving uneven pathways and subdued lighting may not be suitable for travellers with disabilities. Most hotels are low-rise, although some, like the Meridien Barbarons (*see p149*), have three storeys and rooms for travellers with disabilities at ground level, and the Coral Strand (*see p148*) has a lift to take you up five floors. The dedicated resort island destinations, like Desroches (*see pp102–3*), are flat and easy to get around, but check with your travel agent or directly with the hotel before booking.

Desroches Island is relatively flat for travellers with disabilities

Language

There are three official languages in the Seychelles – English, French and Creole (or Kreol). English is widely spoken and understood, and is the language commonly used in business. French is also spoken, although, in practice, many Seychellois prefer to use English with visitors or the lingua franca Creole among themselves. Creole has its roots in French, the language of the masters, and was adapted by slaves of African and Malagasy origin as a common means of communication. Today, it is an official language and earns the same respect as English and French. English-speaking visitors will have no trouble communicating in shops, hotels, banks and restaurants, but a few Creole expressions are always appreciated. If you have a basic knowledge of French, you will recognise some words and phrases, but even as a non-French speaker the language is easy to learn. Some simple basics to observe are that the French 'j' becomes 'z', the French rules of gender don't apply, you don't even need a French accent, and words are pronounced just as they are written.

PHRASES

English	Creole	French
Hello	Bonzour	Bonjour
Goodbye	Orevwar	Au revoir
How are you?	Ki dir?	Comment allez-vous?
Thank you	Mersi	Merci
Where	Kote	Où
Please	Silvouple	S'il vous plaît
I don't understand	Mon pa konpran	Je ne comprends pas
I like it	Mon kontan	Ça me plaît
How are you?	Konman sava?	Comment ça va? (informal)
What is this?	Kisisa?	Qu'est-ce que c'est?

English	Creole	French
He, she, it	Li	Il, elle
OK	Korek	Ça va bien
Not OK	Pas korek	Ça ne va pas bien
Hot water	Oshod	Eau chaude
Bus stop	Bistop	L'arrêt de bus

English	French
What is your name?	Comment vous appellez-vous?
I would like…	Je voudrais…
It's good	C'est bon
How much is it?	Combien ça coûte?
It's expensive	C'est cher
Market	Le marché
Supermarket	Le supermarché
Chemist	La pharmacie
Post office	Le bureau de poste
Stamp	Timbre
Restaurant	Le restaurant
I'm hungry	J'ai faim
I'm thirsty	J'ai soif
Beer	La bière
Wine	Du vin
Tea with milk	Thé au lait
Waiters	Garçons
Hotel	L'hôtel
Towel	Serviette de bain
I'm not well	Je ne me sens pas bien
I need a doctor	J'ai besoin d'un médecin

Emergencies

Emergency telephone number
Police, Fire and Ambulance service: 999

Health risks
There are no serious health risks in the Seychelles and the country is free of malaria, yellow fever, cholera and other tropical diseases. No vaccinations are needed unless you have travelled through a country considered to be a yellow fever area within the last six days prior to your arrival in Seychelles. If you have travelled from South America or Africa (excluding South Africa), you will need to provide a vaccination certificate.

Healthcare
Tap water is safe to drink, and mineral water is widely available in shops, hotels and restaurants. Standards of hygiene in hotels and restaurants meet Western standards, and provided you take the same sensible precautions as you would in your home country, your stay should pass without any serious mishap. Heat exhaustion, sunstroke and tummy problems are common in tropical countries, so avoid staying out in the sun too long, wear a high-factor sunblock, drink plenty of fluids, and make sure that fresh fruit and vegetables are washed before eating.

Medical insurance is always a good idea, if only for the peace of mind it brings knowing that any expenses should be met if you are injured or fall ill. Generic drugs, which may appear under a different name, are available from the private pharmacy in Victoria (*see p138*). Hospitals and health centres have their own dispensaries and all drugs dispensed need a prescription. If you are on prescribed medication, it would be wise to bring enough to cover your needs. Doctors and dentists are listed in the telephone directory. The charges are reasonable and the treatment is usually good. Your hotel can make the necessary arrangements.

Hospitals and health centres
Waiting times can be very long at government hospitals and health centres. The consultation fee is SR100 plus the cost of any prescribed drugs.

Anse Boileau Health Centre
West Mahé. Tel: 355 555.

Anse Royale Hospital
South Mahé. Tel: 371 222.

Baie Sainte Anne Hospital
Praslin. Tel: 232 333.

Beau Vallon Health Centre
Tel: 388 000.

Beoliere Health Centre
West Mahé. Tel: 378 259.

Logan Hospital

La Digue. Tel: 234 255.

Victoria Hospital

Mont Fleuri, Victoria, Mahé. Tel: 388 000.

Crime

Seychelles is a low-risk destination, and any crime that does take place tends to be opportunistic. People are generally honest, but, as in other parts of the world, don't leave valuables unattended, especially on the beach. There are touts operating around Beau Vallon who may ask if you are looking for rupees. Changing money on the black market is illegal and if you are caught you could land in trouble.

Embassies

If you are arrested or need legal representation, contact your diplomatic representative. The nearest foreign missions for nationals of Canada, Australia, New Zealand and South Africa are in Mauritius.

Australia High Commission

2nd floor, Rogers House, President John Kennedy Street, Port Louis, Mauritius. Tel: (230) 202 0160.

British High Commission

Oliaji Trade Centre, Victoria, Mahé. Tel: (248) 283 666.

Canada High Commission

c/o Blanche Birger Company Ltd, 8 Jules Koenig Street, Port Louis, Mauritius. Tel: (230) 212 5500.

New Zealand Consulate

Anchor Building, Les Pailles, Mauritius. Tel: (230) 286 4920.

South Africa High Commission

4th floor, BAI Building, Pope Hennessy Street, Port Louis, Mauritius. Tel: (230) 212 6925.

United States Consulate

Oliaji Trade Centre, Victoria, Mahé. Tel: (248) 222 256.

Happy-go-lucky firemen on Denis Island

Directory

Accommodation price guide

Accommodation can be paid in local or foreign currency.	**£**	up to £300
Major credit cards, such as Visa, MasterCard and	**££**	£300–600
American Express, are acceptable. Prices shown are based	**£££**	£600–800
on a double room per night for two people sharing.	**££££**	above £800

Eating out price guide

	£	up to SR100 (£5)
Prices are based on an average two-course	**££**	SR100–SR150 (£5–7)
meal per head, without drinks.	**£££**	SR150–SR200 (£7–9)
	££££	above SR200 (£9)

MAHÉ

Anse Faure

ENTERTAINMENT

Katiolo Night Club

More a disco than a nightclub, although live performances turn up now and again. Enjoy hip hop and rhythm and blues to while away the evening. Wednesday is Ladies' Night.
Tel: 375 453. Open: Wed–Sat 10pm–3am. Admission charge.

Anse Intendance

ACCOMMODATION

Banyan Tree ££££

Spacious villas with private pools cling to the hillsides of this 'A' list celebrity haunt. Grand colonial-style public areas with lots of terraces and an à la carte restaurant complement the spa, gym and infinity pool.
Tel: 383 500.
Fax: 383 600.
www.banyantree.com

Anse à la Mouche

ACCOMMODATION

Blue Lagoon Chalets £

This is a modern two-bedroom bungalow complex set in gardens. Each chalet has a well-equipped kitchen, large lounge, air conditioning, a safe and a TV, appealing to self-catering families seeking an independent beach-based holiday. Daily maid service and cook on request.
Tel: 371 197.
Fax: 371 565.
Email: blagoon @seychelles.net.
www.seychelles.net/ bluelagoon

Anse aux Pins

EATING OUT

Vye Marmit ££

A pleasant restaurant catering to tour groups visiting the Craft Village. It specialises in Creole fare but is also good for snacks.
Domaine de Val des Près Craft Village.
Tel: 376 155. Open: Mon–Sat 11am–9pm.

Mare Sport Ltd (Glass-bottom boat trips)
Tel: 376 814.
www.maresportsltd.com
Seychelles Golf Club
Nine-hole golf course on coconut plantation.
Tel: 376 234. Email:
edwin@seychelles.sc.
www.seychellesgolfclub.
com. Open: daily; booking
recommended for Sat.

Anse Royale
Jardin du Roi ££
Traditional curries, savoury pancakes and sweet pancakes topped with cinnamon ice cream all feature on the menu. This is part of the Jardin du Roi estate with lovely views over the east coast.
Tel: 371 313.
Open: 10am–5.30pm.

Coral Magic Ltd (Glass-bottom boat trips)
Tel: 510 412.

Anse Soleil
Anse Soleil Beachcomber £
Secluded, slightly quirky hideaway of 14 rooms, each with a safe, fridge and coffee-making facilities. The colourful dining room and adjacent public café lend local atmosphere, while coastal and inland walks appeal to budget-conscious visitors.
Tel: 361 461. Fax: 361 460.
www.beachcomber.sc

Anse Takamaka
Chez Batista Bungalows £
Charming bungalow beachfront complex tucked in a quiet corner of one of Mahé's most beautiful beaches. The comfortable accommodation includes tea- and coffee-making facilities, TV, air conditioning and fan.
Tel: 366 300. Email:
batistas@seychelles.net.
www.chez-batista.com
South Point Chalets ££
Modern self-catering apartments set in a verdant valley, appealing to independent travellers. Car hire available.
Tel: 366 484. Email:
info@southpointchalets.sc.
www.southpointchalets.sc

Barbarons
Le Meridien Barbarons Hotel
Live entertainment every night in the buzzing bar includes *crazz* – a fusion of Creole music and jazz, as well as soul and pop music.
Tel: 673 000.
Open: 8.30–11.30pm.
Free admission.

Utegangar Riding Centre (Horse riding)
Book lessons and excursions here.
Utegangar Riding Centre.
Tel: 712 355.

Baie Lazare
Four Seasons Seychelles ££££
Traditional French colonial architecture meets Creole charm in this luxurious 67-villa resort carved out of a steep jungly hillside and overlooking the castaway beach. Hilltop spa, kids club and gourmet restaurants.
Tel: 393 000.
Fax: 393 001. www.
fourseasons.com/seychelles

Beau Vallon

ACCOMMODATION

Augerine Hotel £

Friendly, family-run colonial-style hotel with 15 simple en-suite air-conditioned rooms in a prime beach location. Evening meals are cooked to order.
Tel/fax: 247 257. Email: augerine@seychelles.sc. www.augerinehotel.com

Beau Vallon Bungalows £

Charming family-owned self-catering bungalows and double rooms, behind the beach and centrally located for food shops, bars and restaurants. Fishing boat trips, car hire and excursions can be arranged.
Tel: 247 382 or 247 376. Fax: 247 955. Email: bvbung@seychelles.net. www.beauvallonbungalows. com

Coral Strand Hotel £

Russian management and 2009 refurb of this centrally located beachfront hotel attract couples and families looking for fun in the sun. Comfortable rooms, buffet, bistro, Indian restaurant and beach bar plus lively pool area.
Tel: 621 000. Fax: 247 517. Email: mail@coralstrand.sc. www.coralstrand.com

Hanneman Holiday Residence £

Delightful self-catering apartments with all mod cons in secure walled complex with pool and pretty gardens owned by former manager of Coral Strand Hotel. Ideal for couples and families and within walking distance of beach, shops and bus stop.
Tel: 425 000. Fax: 425 010. http://hanneman-seychelles.com

EATING OUT

The Boat House ££££

There is an all-you-can-eat buffet in this buzzing hangout. Wholesome curries, fish of the day, salads to die for and coconut desserts. Booking essential.
Beau Vallon beach. Tel: 247 898. www.boathouse.sc. Open: Evenings only for 7.30pm prompt start.

Mahek ££££

Master chefs prepare food in the show kitchen of this sophisticated Indian restaurant. Try hot curries, biryanis and tandoori specialities. Booking recommended.
Coral Strand Hotel. Tel: 621 000 extension 835. www.coralstrand.com. Open: noon–2pm, 7–9.45pm. Closed: Tue.

ENTERTAINMENT

Berjaya Beau Vallon Hotel

Local crooners and traditional Seychellois bands provide nightly music in the bar for guests and non-guests.
Beau Vallon beach. Tel: 287 287. Open: 7pm–midnight. Free admission.

Coral Strand Hotel

Popular haunt for locals who join guests around the pool for traditional and Western music. Tuesday jazz nights are recommended.
Beau Vallon beach. Tel: 621 000. Every night from 7.30–10pm. Free admission.

SPORT AND LEISURE

Cycling

You'll find bicycles for hire at Beau Vallon on

Mahé, Côte d'Or and Grande Anse on Praslin and many in town on La Digue. Expect to pay around SR50 per hour. On the more remote islands, a bike often comes free with your accommodation or can be hired direct from the resort.

Basil Beaudouin (Hiking)
Knowledgeable private guide with years of experience under his belt.
c/o Coral Strand Hotel. Tel: 241 790.

Beau Vallon Aquatic Sport
Motorised watersports including banana rides and waterskiing.
Tel: 594 367.

Big Blue Divers
Mare Anglaise. Tel: 261 106. www.bigbluedivers.net

Dive Seychelles
Berjaya Beau Vallon Beach Hotel. Tel: 247 165. www.diveseychelles.com.sc

Dani's Boat Charter
Big-game fishing, marine park excursions, inter-island trips and

individual tours can be arranged here.
Tel: 414 036 or 525 200.

Leisure 2000 (Water-sports)
Full range of water-sports including pedalos, canoeing, windsurfing and sailing equipment.
Tel: 594 367.

Striker Ltd (Fishing)
Half- and full-day fishing trips to Praslin, La Digue and Silhouette.
Coral Strand Hotel. Tel: 511 958 or 247 848.

Teddy's Glass Bottom (Boat trips)
Tel: 261 125 or 511 125. Email: teddysgbb@yahoo.com

Bel Ombre
ACCOMMODATION
Meridien Fisherman's Cove ££££
All 70 rooms are sea-facing and luxuriously appointed with open bathrooms and private terrace. You can enjoy complimentary afternoon tea, romantic restaurants, a late-night bar, a stunning infinity pool and impeccable service.

Tel: 677 000. Fax: 620 900. www.lemeridien.com/ fishcove

SPORT AND LEISURE
For details and venues of sporting and leisure events contact:
Seychelles Tourist Information Office
Victoria, Mahé. Tel: 610 800.

Glacis
EATING OUT
Hilltop Restaurant ££££
Mahé's most sophisticated restaurant is noted for stylish international and local cuisine and magnificent ocean views. Booking recommended.
Northolme Hotel and Spa. Tel: 290 000. Open: For lunch and dinner.

Grande Anse
ACCOMMODATION
Meridien Barbarons Hotel £££
Large, busy beach hotel with contemporary-style rooms built around a 25m (82ft) lap pool and popular with package holiday tourists. There are three restaurants, sporting facilities and nightly entertainment.

Tel: 673 000. Fax: 673 352.
www.lemeridien.com/
barbarons

Port Glaud

ACCOMMODATION

Eden's Holiday Villas £

Ten self-catering
apartments overlooking
Port Glaud, close to a bus
stop and the beach.
Tel: 378 333. Email:
eden@seychelles.net. www.
thesunsethotelgroup.com

Victoria

TOURIST INFORMATION

Independence House,
Victoria. Tel: 610 800.
Open: Mon–Fri
8am–5pm, Sat 9am–noon.

TOUR OPERATORS

The following Mahé-
based tour operators
offer a full range of
excursions, itineraries,
flights and
accommodation.

7 Degrees South

Kingsgate Travel Centre,
Independence Avenue,
Victoria. Tel: 292 800.
Email:
7south@seychelles.net.
www.7south.net

Creole Travel Services

Orion House, Victoria.
Tel: 297 000. Email: info@
creoletravelservices.com.
www.creoletravelservices.
com

Masons Travel

Michel Building,
Revolution Avenue,
Victoria. Tel: 288 888.
Email:
info@masonstravel.com.
www.masonstravel.com

EATING OUT

News Café £

In the old part of town,
this restaurant overlooks
Market Street from the
first-floor terrace. Grab
breakfast or a lunch of
fresh salad and well-filled
sandwiches in
contemporary
surroundings.
Trinity House, Albert
Street. Tel: 322 999.
Closed: Evenings.

Pirates Arms ££

Enjoy decent coffee and a
pastry or tuck into Creole
and international cuisine
in this popular restaurant
in the heart of Victoria.
Pirates Arms Building,
Independence Avenue.
Tel: 225 001.
Open: 9am–midnight.

Le Rendezvous ★★

Fill up on pasta, fish
kebabs or filleted red
snapper dishes in this
first-floor restaurant
overlooking the
Clock Tower.
Francis Rachel Street.
Tel: 323 556.
Open: 9am–midnight.
Closed: Sun.

Marie-Antoinette ££££

There is a set menu of
Creole fare in this
colonial-style restaurant.
Dip into chicken and fish
curries, white rice,
vegetables and salad, and
enjoy the views of the
Sainte Anne Marine Park.
St Louis. Tel: 266 222.
Open: noon–2.30pm &
6.30–9pm. Closed: Sun.

ENTERTAINMENT

Deepam (Cinema)

Deepam Cinema, in
town and at Docklands
near the waterfront,
shows the latest English-
language films in
Victoria. Turn up and
buy your ticket on the
day or telephone first.
Albert Street and at
Docklands. Tel: 610 197
or 610 399.
www.deepamsey.com

Love Nut Night Club

Meet the locals and
gyrate to Western pop
music hits. Wednesday
night is Ladies' Night,

and Sunday sees Happy Hour and another session of bopping.
Premier Building, Albert Street, Victoria.
Tel: 323 795.
Open: Wed, Fri, Sat 10.30pm–5am.
Admission charge.

Pirates Arms
Enjoy a meal and listen to *crazz*, crooners, Western pop and traditional bands performing in the restaurant every night from 7pm onwards.
Pirates Arms Building, Independence Avenue.
Tel: 225 001.

Theatre
There are no English-language performances, but occasional plays and shows in Creole are shown at the **Creole Institute** (*Tel: 376 351*) and in French at the **Alliance Française** (*Tel: 282 424*). Consult the tourist office for details.

FESTIVALS AND EVENTS
There is no central ticket agency for events such as the Kreol Festival, SUBIOS Underwater Festival and Fetafrik

(*see pp20–21*). Most activities are free anyway and take place in the street or in hotels. Where paying activities are involved, say for screenings of film or performances, consult the tourist office for further details.

SPORT AND LEISURE
Many small operators provide glass-bottom boats to Sainte Anne and Baie Ternay Marine Parks. The trip includes barbecue lunch, soft drinks and snorkelling equipment. Half-day trips also available and some offer trips to Cerf Island too.

Angel Fish Yacht Charter
This company provides crewed, bare-boat and day charters, fishing around the Inner Islands and fly fishing in the Outer Islands as well as snorkelling and diving.
Roche Caiman.
Eden Island, Mahé.
Tel: 344 644. www.seychelles-charter.com

Cerf Island Explorer
For personalised diving in Sainte Anne

National Marine Park.
Tel 570 043. Email: pal@seychelles.net

Elegant Yachting
This operator provides crewed, bare-boat and/or day charters.
Eden Island, Marine House, Victoria.
Tel: 515 736.
www.elegant-yachting.com

Hiking
A list of hiking guides can be obtained from the Botanical Gardens.
Mont Fleuri Road, Victoria.
Tel: 670 500.

Indian Ocean Explorer (Cruising)
Indian Ocean Explorer II is undergoing a refit and is expected to start operating 2011. Bookings can be made through:
Voyage of Discovery GmbH in Switzerland.
Tel: (33) 6 2104 0050.
Fax: (41) 4 4567 1938.
Email: catherine@ioexpl.com.
www.ioexpl.com

Masons Travel (Hiking)
For organised inland and coastal hikes in Mahé, Praslin and La Digue.
Revolution Avenue,

Victoria. Tel: 288 888.
www.masonstravel.com
Silhouette Cruises
This operator provides
crewed live-aboard
cruises and charters
aboard Dutch top-sail
schooner or modern
yachts. Expeditions
on oceanographic
vessel MV *Maya's
Dugong*.
Tel: 324 026. Email:
cruises@seychelles.net.
www.seychelles-
cruises.com

PRASLIN
TOURIST INFORMATION
Praslin Airport, Amitie.
Tel: 233 346.
Open: Mon–Fri
8am–5pm & Sat
8am–noon (public
holidays 8am–1pm).
Closed: Sun.
Also a small office on
the jetty at Baie
Sainte Anne.
Open: To coincide with
boat arrivals/departures.

Anse Bois de Rose
SPORT AND LEISURE
**Charming Lady
(Cruising)**
This operator provides
crewed, bare-boat and/or
day charters.

Freroc Ltd, c/o Hotel Coco
de Mer. Tel: 290 555.
www.cocodemer.com

Anse Gouvernement
SPORT AND LEISURE
Corsair Boat Charter
c/o Hotel L'Archipel. Tel:
232 138. Email:
bigarade@Seychelles.net.
www.bigarade.net

Anse Kerlan
ACCOMMODATION
Lemuria Resort ££££
Bounded by pristine
beaches and an 18-hole
golf course, this is
Praslin's best hotel, with
spacious accommodation
and service with a smile.
For a special occasion,
book a two-bedroom villa
that includes private pool,
sunken dining area, and a
villa master to take care of
all your needs. The buffet
restaurant overlooks
tiered pools, and there's
fine dining and local
cuisine.
Tel: 281 281. Fax: 281 001.
www.lemuriaresort.com

SPORT AND LEISURE
**Lemuria Resort Golf
Course**
Seychelles' only 18-hole
golf course. Open to non-

residents but phone first
to book a green fee.
Tel: 281 281. Fax 281 001.
Email:
resa@lemuriaresort.com.
www.lemuriaresort.com

Anse Lazio
EATING OUT
Le Chevalier ££
Sumptuous seafood
and delicious fish curries
in this casual beachside
restaurant that offers a
stunning view.
Tel: 232 322. Open: daily
8am–4pm.

Anse Volbert
SPORT AND LEISURE
Octopus Diving Centre
Tel: 232 602. Email:
octopus@seychelles.net.
www.octopusdiver.com
Whitetip Divers
Paradise Sun Hotel.
Tel: 232 282.
www.whitetipdivers.com

Baie Sainte Anne
EATING OUT
Coco Rouge Takeaway £
Cheap snacks and take-
aways in handy
containers are sold here –
just right for a lazy picnic
on the beach.
Tel: 232 228. Open: For
lunch and dinner.

ENTERTAINMENT
Oxygene (Nightclub)
Disco with special appearances by local artistes where islanders let their hair down.
Tel: 512 300. Open: Fri & Sat 10pm–4am. Admission charge.

SPORT AND LEISURE
Dream Yacht Seychelles
Provides crewed, bareboat and/or day charters.
Tel: 232 681. www.dream-yacht-seychelles.com
Summer's Day (Cruising)
Provides crewed, bareboat and/or day charters.
Freroc Ltd, c/o Hotel Coco de Mer. Tel: 290 555. www.cocodemer.com

Cap Samy
SPORT AND LEISURE
Victorin Laboudallon (Hiking)
Personalised nature walks with former conservation officer.
Tel: 513 370.

Côte d'Or
ACCOMMODATION
Acajou Hotel ££
Built of acajou, a dark mahogany wood from South Africa, this two-storey colonial-style beach complex is set in a U-shape amid a jungle of vegetation. The 28 rooms are cool and spacious and have satellite TV, minibar and a safe. Charming staff and friendly service.
Tel: 232 400. Fax: 232 401. www.acajouhotel.com
Le Duc de Praslin ££
Welcoming family-run complex of 24 luxuriously appointed rooms and suites. Up to five people can stay in the family suite, which has two bedrooms, a grand living area and spacious veranda. There's a decked freeform pool, alfresco restaurant, and it's a short stroll to the beach.
Anse Volbert. Tel: 294 800. Fax: 232 355. www.leduc-seychelles.com
Hotel L'Archipel ££
Sophisticated colonial-style hillside accommodation of 30 rooms and suites with easy walkways to a fine beach. There are free canoes, snorkelling equipment and windsurfing facilities, a large decked pool and an à la carte restaurant.
Anse Gouvernement. Tel: 284 700. Fax: 232 072. www.larchipel.com
Villas d'Or ££
Self-catering accommodation comprising ten villas beside the beach provides home-from-home comfort on a grand scale. All villas have kitchen, air conditioning, TV and video, a safe, and maid service. There is free evening transport to nearby restaurants.
Tel: 232 777. Fax: 232 505. Email: villador@seychelles.net. www.seychelles.net/villador

EATING OUT
Tante Mimi £££
Colonial-style villa with Creole and international meals served in the restaurant on the first floor, with a casino below. Book ahead.
Casino des Isles, midway between Villas d'Or and Hotel L'Archipel. Tel: 232 500. Open: daily 7.30–11pm.

SPORT AND LEISURE

Côte d'Or Bicycle Hire
Tel: 232 071.

Grande Anse

ACCOMMODATION

Britannia Hotel £
This family-run
12-room hotel is a
good budget option for
independent visitors
and is centrally located
for the village.
It has a small pool, an
excellent restaurant that
serves Creole food, and
day trips to Aride and
other islands can be
arranged.
Tel: 233 215.
Fax: 233 944.
www.seychelles-resa.com

Indian Ocean Lodge £
There's a nice casual
feel about this complex
nestling in verdant
gardens. Thirty-two
bright rooms each
have a four-poster bed,
TV, safe, fridge and
tea/coffee-making
facilities. The rustic
restaurant serves great
food and poolside
snacks. Seaweed build-up
is a problem during
the southeast monsoon,
but a free daily shuttle
to Côte d'Or beach is
available for guests.
Tel: 233 324. Fax: 233 911.
Email: iol@seychelles.net.
www.indianoceanlodge.com

Villa de Mer £
This cheerful collection
of sea-facing bungalows
has stunning views of
Cousin and Cousine
Islands. Well-furnished,
ten-room accommodation
includes a plantation-
style house overlooking
the resort's lap pool.
There is a pleasant
restaurant/bar and a
welcoming family-run
atmosphere. The bus
stops right outside.
Amitie. Tel: 233 972.
Fax: 233 015.
Email: vdemer@seychelles.
net. www.seychelles-
holidays.com

EATING OUT

Britannia Restaurant £££
Talented family chef
prepares octopus curry,
freshly grated pawpaw
pickle and chutneys, and
melt-in-the-mouth red
snapper. Booking
recommended, especially
for Sunday lunch.
Britannia Hotel.
Tel: 233 215. Fax: 233 944.
Open: noon–2.30pm,
7.30–9.30pm.

ENTERTAINMENT

Wahoo Bar
Located inside the Indian
Ocean Lodge Hotel, this
convivial bar offers
entertainment twice a
week and is a popular
meeting place for exotic
cocktails, drinks and
tasty snacks.
Tel: 233 324. Open:
daily 10am–11pm.
Admission charge.

SPORT AND LEISURE

Makaira (Fishing)
Beach Villa Guesthouse.
Tel: 521 515. Email:
makaira@email.sc.
www.beach-villa-
sportfishing.com

**Praslin Touring
(Hiking)**
Personalised tour by
expert Michael Jean-
Louis in Vallée
de Mai.
Tel: 524 150. Email:
mejeanlouis@seychelles.net

Côte d'Or

SPORT AND LEISURE

VIP Tour (Hiking)
Local expert Umberto
Ugo Sala offers hiking
throughout beautiful
Praslin landscapes.
Tel: 770 966. E-mail:
viptour@seychelles.sc

Pointe Cabris
ACCOMMODATION
Château de Feuilles ££
A ten-room hideaway
where guests are treated
with courtesy and charm.
Perched on a cliff top,
the accommodation is
superbly appointed.
The cosy restaurant and
bar and 15m (49ft) lap
pool overlook sea and
gardens, and a hilltop
jacuzzi gives 360-degree
views of satellite islands.
There are boat and dive
excursions and a free
car-hire package.
Tel: 290 000. Fax: 290 029.
Email: info@
chateaudefeuilles.com.
www.
chateaudefeuilles.com

SPORT AND LEISURE
Oceanic Ventures
(Fishing)
Tel: 232 315. Email:
oceanic@seychelles.net

LA DIGUE
Anse Patate
ACCOMMODATION
Patatran Village £
Eighteen simple
bungalows built on a
steep hillside, with an
impressive reception,
swimming pool, bar

and an à la carte
restaurant overlooking
sandy coves.
Tel: 294 300.
Fax: 294 390.
www.patatranseychelles.
com

Anse Réunion
ACCOMMODATION
La Digue Island
Lodge ££
Popular with families,
honeymooners and
couples, with an eclectic
range of accommodation
in spacious grounds. The
hotel can also organise
fishing and snorkelling
trips to neighbouring
islands, sunset cruises,
nature walks, trekking,
cycling and horseriding
in nearby L'Union Estate.
Tel: 292 525. Fax: 234 132.
www.ladigue.sc

SPORT AND LEISURE
La Fidelité
Snorkelling and barbecues
with qualified skipper.
Tel: 234 237.
Email:
lafidelite@seychelles.sc
Zico 1 Boat Charter
(Fishing)
Tel: 515 557.
Email: nevis_ernesta@
hotmail.com

Anse Source d'Argent
EATING OUT
Lanbousir £
Kick off your shoes and
rub your toes in the
sand-covered interior
of this thatched-roof
café serving sandwiches,
salads and yummy
cakes.
No telephone.
Open: 10am–5pm.

SPORT AND LEISURE
L'Union Estate
(Horse riding)
You can hire a horse for
rides inside the fenced
area of L'Union Estate
or along Anse Source
d'Argent beach.
L'Union Estate.
Tel: 234 240.
Open: Mon–Fri
8am–3pm.
Rates are charged
per hour.

Grande Anse
EATING OUT
Loutier Coco ££
Authentic Creole buffet
spread in this simple
sand-floor eatery within
easy walking distance of
the beach.
Tel: 514 762. Open:
Mon–Sat 12.30–3pm, Sun
12.30–3pm & for dinner.

La Passe

EATING OUT

Chez Marston £

This is the perfect place for people-watching while you enjoy a delicious omelette or tasty sandwich on the picturesque terrace. All this is just a stone's throw from the town.
Tel: 234 023. Open: For lunch and dinner.

SPORT AND LEISURE

Belle Petra (Cruising)

This operator provides half- and full-day trips on a catamaran to neighbouring islands. Excursions include birdwatching and snorkelling.
Tel: 234 302. Email: petra@seychelles.sc

Lone Wolf Charters (Fishing)
Tel: 570 344.

Michelin Bicycle Hire
Tel: 234 304.

Tati's Hire (Bicycles)
Tel: 234 346.

TOURIST INFORMATION
La Passe. Tel: 234 393. Open: Mon–Fri 8am–5pm, Sat 9am–noon (public holidays 9am–noon). Closed: Sun.

Patatran

EATING OUT

Patatran Village Restaurant £££

This well-located restaurant offers an extensive menu featuring the local island soup, jack fish, job fish or lobster, and a laid-back local ambience in this idyllic timber-clad sea-facing location.
Tel: 294 300. Open: noon–2.30pm, 7–9.30pm.

BIRD ISLAND

SPORT AND LEISURE

Bird Island Ltd (Fishing)

Game- and bottom-fishing specialist on Bird Island resort for the marine-rich waters of Seychelles Bank.
Bird Island. Tel: 224 925. www.birdislandseychelles. com

DENIS ISLAND

SPORT AND LEISURE

Denis Island Sportfishing

Deep-sea angling and big-game fishing operator on Denis Island.
Denis Island. Tel: 321 143. Email: denis@seychelles.net

NORTH ISLAND

SPORT AND LEISURE

North Island Dive Centre
North Island. Tel: 293 100. www.north-island.com

OUTER ISLANDS

SPORT AND LEISURE

Frontiers International Travel

These fly-fishing specialists offer trips to Alphonse, Bijoutier and Saint François Islands. This company is American-based, but there is a UK office.
Frontiers Travel, Kennet Cottage, Kempford, Gloucestershire GL7 4EQ. Tel: 0845 299 6212. Fax: 01285 700 322. Email: info@frontierstrvl.co.uk. www.frontierstravel.com

Ocean Charters

Big-game, fly-fishing, deep-sea fishing, bone fishing and overnight charters to Amirantes and beyond.
305 AARTI Chambers, Mont Fleuri, Mahé. Tel: 321 100 or 711 100. Fax: 321 142. Email: info@oceancharters.sc. www.oceancharters.sc

Index

Acknowledgements

The author wishes to thank the following organisations for their kind hospitality and assistance in the preparation of this guide: Seychelles Tourist Board, Coral Strand Hotel, The Hilton Seychelles Northolme Resort, The Plantation Hotel, The Banyan Tree Resort, Cerf Island Resort and Anse Soleil Beachcomber Hotel in Mahé, Lemuria Resort, Indian Ocean Lodge, Coco de Mer Hotel and Château de Feuilles Hotel in Praslin, La Digue Island Resort on La Digue, Denis Island Resort and Desroches Island Resort in the Outer Islands, Jessica Giroux of Masons Travel, Lindsay Chong-Seng of The Seychelles Islands Foundation and Jimmy Mancienne at The Boat House in Mahé.

Thomas Cook Publishing wishes to thank ERIC ROBERTS, to whom the copyright belongs, for the photographs in this book, except for the following images:

SEYCHELLES TOURIST BOARD 16, 19, 20 (Johnathan Smith/Sunsail), 21, 41, 52 (Angelo Cavalli), 69 (Paul Turcotte), 71 (Angelo Cavalli), 72 (Bharath Ramamruthan), 73 (Frank Schneider), 95 (Angelo Cavalli), 99 (Paul Turcotte), 110, 111 (Andrea Maggi); ANGELFISH DIVING 106, 107; BANYAN TREE HOTELS AND RESORTS 94; TAJ DENIS ISLAND 83, 122; LA DIGUE ISLAND LODGE/PAUL TURCOTTE 23, 80, 81; WORLD PICTURES 50, 56, 108; PICTURES COLOUR LIBRARY 55; FREGATE ISLAND PRIVATE 93, 109; THOMAS COOK 8; DREAMSTIME.COM 1 (Nikolais), 25 (Walter Quirtmair), 47 (Gator), 48 (Sapsiwai), 113 (Paul Cowan); iSTOCKPHOTO 42 (DJM aftaar), 70 (Rainer von Brandis)

For CAMBRIDGE PUBLISHING MANAGEMENT LIMITED:
Project editor: Jennifer Jahn
Typesetter: Paul Queripel
Copy editor: Jo Osborn
Proofreaders: Jan McCann & Michele Greenbank
Indexer: Karolin Thomas

SEND YOUR THOUGHTS TO BOOKS@THOMASCOOK.COM

We're committed to providing the very best up-to-date information in our travel guides and constantly strive to make them as useful as they can be. You can help us to improve future editions by letting us have your feedback. If you've made a wonderful discovery on your travels that we don't already feature, if you'd like to inform us about recent changes to anything that we do include, or if you simply want to let us know your thoughts about this guidebook and how we can make it even better – we'd love to hear from you.

Send us ideas, discoveries and recommendations today and then look out for your valuable input in the next edition of this title.

Emails to the above address, or letters to the traveller guides Series Editor, Thomas Cook Publishing, PO Box 227, Coningsby Road, Peterborough PE3 8SB, UK.

Please don't forget to let us know which title your feedback refers to!